Nothing could be more importa[...] tation than the unfolding of a new cosmolog[...] unified Universe to reveal itself as a single, integrated, spiritual whole.

Where did we come from? Why are we here? Where are we going? In this fascinating volume, women and men of our time consider the timeless questions of existence to illuminate that place where our religious yearnings and scientific understanding meet.

– JOHN SEED

I have come to an understanding of the sacredness of all life through my work to end government killing. This sacredness underlies each article in this book, giving a new vision of hope and meaning to life.

– HELEN PREJEAN

Important reading for all who want to explore the interface between new, scientific understandings of the universe and their personal spiritual journey. In this work Jim Schenk interweaves his own spiritual quest with well-selected insights from some key thinkers on questions such as "Who or What is God in an expanding and evolving universe?" "Why are we here?" "What does it mean to be human?" "Where are we going?" and "What happens after death?" Such questions of ultimacy and meaning are at the heart of all authentic religions, but responders in this volume go beyond old, limited concepts and open new pathways of wisdom illuminated by the new cosmology. Every page informs and inspires. I will revisit this collection often and share it with others.

– PAT MISCHE

"In this thought provoking collection, Jim Schenk invites us to step into the flowing river of exploration and experience of Spirit. Tribal people recognize Spirit in everything; it is heartening to read the courageous words of those in the west who know the sacred "in their bones" as well as in their theology"

– MALIDOMA PATRICE SOMÉ

"St. Thomas Aquinas, one of the Church's greatest theologians, wrote 750 years ago, "A mistake about Creation will result in a mistake about God." What Does God Look Like In An Expanding Universe *offers fresh, evolutionary thinking from creative minds and hearts across the theological spectrum about some of life's big questions: Where did we come from? Why are we here? Where are we going? What is the nature of ultimate reality? What happens after death? To say this book is timely would be a serous understatement!"*

– MICHAEL DOWD

WHAT DOES
GOD
LOOK LIKE
IN AN EXPANDING UNIVERSE?

EDITED BY

Jim Schenk

ImagoEarth Publishing
Cincinnati, Ohio

IMAGO EARTH PUBLISHING

ISBN-10: 0–61513–079–8
ISBN-13: 978-0-615-13079-8
Library of Congress Control Number: 2006900818

Jacket and book design by Michael J. Frazier

Illustrations by Marion C. Honors, C. S. J.

Printed in USA on recycled paper.

To my family: my wife Eileen, children Megan and Devin, their spouses Matt and Jill and our beautiful grandchildren Nathan, Laura and Kathleen for their help in deepening my love for the Earth and my understanding of our interconnectedness with this magnificent planet. We are Earth.

CONTENTS

PART ONE: **Where Did We Come From?**

CHAPTER ONE: A PERSONAL PERSPECTIVE

PART TWO: Why Are We Here?

CHAPTER THREE: A PERSONAL PERSPECTIVE

CHAPTER FOUR: A UNIVERSAL PERSPECTIVE

PART THREE: Where Are We Going?

CHAPTER FIVE: A PERSONAL PERSPECTIVE

ACKNOWLEDGMENTS

To my sister Janet Schenk who spent countless hours helping me with all the details of the book; Catherine Browning for helping me revise the book, edit and write for it; Michael Frazier for his wonderful gift of doing the layout of the book; Kim Marcum, Joyce Quinlan and Dave Glober for editing; Judith Boice for help getting started in producing this book; for the authors who so willingly produced their articles for the book; Eileen who proofread the book and put up with "the mess."

Coming to Terms

I was born in 1943 and grew up in a large, devout Catholic family on a small farm in Southern Indiana. As one of 11 children, I attended Catholic Mass every day starting at the age of six. With two brothers who were priests and three sisters who were women religious, it was assumed that I would follow my brothers into the priesthood. As expected, I went into the seminary at the age of fourteen and spent the next ten years of my life there.

In 1966, in my ninth year at seminary and at the age of twenty-three, I recall studying Sartre, a French philosopher and atheist. I asked my professor, "Why would anyone choose not to believe in God? The alternative of total lack of meaning seems unbearable." Looking back, I realize that those were my only comprehensible choices – a belief in the transcendent God of the Catholic religious tradition or a belief in no God at all.

My college philosophy classes were very exciting. Reading Plato, Aristotle, Augustine, and Aquinas put my theological beliefs into perspective. Philosophers were magnificent examples of where theology can go with the cosmology of the day. I was in awe of their wisdom.

A year later, Cosmology 101 proved to be one of the most life-changing courses I took in graduate school. Having been taught traditional Catholic cosmology in a Catholic seminary, I now was exposed to many new possibilities. The class was taught by a priest who was years ahead of his time. He began with Plato and Aristotle, but quickly moved to Teilhard de Chardin, the Big Bang, the expanding universe, and theories of time/space. For the first time in my life, I began to question my beliefs about where humans come from, why we are here, and where we are going. I began to see that we have more than two choices.

I left the seminary in 1967, not because of faith reasons, but because I was not happy there. I still dreamed of being a priest, but decided to take some reflection and discovery time to determine whether my unhappiness might be due to my surroundings or to deeper stirrings within myself. Over the next year, I completed my master's degree in theology, trained VISTAS (Volunteers in Service to America) and became a social worker, stationed in an urban neighborhood house. Over the next few years, I received a master's degree in social work and worked in the inner city as a social worker. It was the late 60s, a time of high energy and excitement, both culturally and personally. I began a new life that carried a great deal of meaning for me, and my desire to become a priest waned.

During my years as a social worker, a question kept coming to me: "Why, in the wealthiest nation in the world, are there still so many poor people?" And as I spent time with VISTA volunteers, fellow students, staff members and volunteers, and even with friends, I became keenly aware of a pervasive sadness and discontent that seemed to burden the lives of so many people. My research on the issue found that a large percentage of both rich and poor people in this affluent society are unhappy. I began to ask the question "Why?" and wondered about a possible connection regarding the commonality of dissatisfaction in the ranks of both the poor and the wealthy.

Away from the seminary, my quest for more happiness became manifest as I met and married Eileen. Together, we began to seriously pursue the questions that haunted us. After considerable research, thought, and discussion, we concluded that the basic values of the culture, which are related to materialism, consumerism, and monetary gain, are actually contrary to the basic needs of humans. Humans need *connection* – to love and be loved, to care for others and to be cared for. If these basic needs are met, the desire for money and consumer goods is unfulfilling, and having these things does not result in more happiness. On the contrary, the competition that ordinarily accompanies the pursuit of riches frequently draws people away from real human love and caring.

In 1977, I left my director's position at the neighborhood center to explore the subject of human happiness. Eileen and I sponsored myriad workshops and presentations and attended many others that related to "living the good life." In 1978, a friend of ours who was doing coursework on future studies moved in with us. She encountered groups such as Findhorn, Chinook Learning Center, Pendle Hill, and others that were linking spirituality and ecology, and were developing a way of life based upon the most unifying and sustainable aspects of these concepts. Our friend's perspective opened up a whole new arena for us as we looked at not only the alienation from each other that humans experience, but also the virtual human disconnection from the planet. We began to look at poverty, unhappiness, consumerism, and materialism in a whole new way.

The spiritual component underlying the beliefs and actions of these progressive groups became the focus of our work. Our findings brought a new perspective on the questions of where we come from, who are we, and where are we going. Through literature and personal contacts, we became aware of the philosophies of such people as Thomas Berry, David Spangler, Joanna Macy, William Irwin Thompson, Sun Bear, and many others. We attended workshops and sponsored conferences, hosting people who had an ecology/spirituality orientation. It became quite evident to us that happiness, and the fulfillment of human needs, are related to our reconnection to the planet.

This framework led us deeper into the new cosmology and into the new story about where we come from and where we are going. Our insights then led to our development and subsequent launching in 1978 of IMAGO, an ecological education organization in Cincinnati, Ohio. IMAGO has since become the foundation for a large number of workshops and presentations on the subjects of ecology, spirituality, and sustainability; our work to preserve the habitat of species that share this planet with us; and our work to involve and influence our urban neighborhood to take ecology seriously. We want our area of Cincinnati to become a model urban eco-village.

In all the work we have done, spirituality has been at its core. As we develop an ecologically conscious neighborhood, we are aware of the need to ground our work in a spiritual base. This perspective has influenced our work in both preserving land and in seeing the spiritual connection between Earth and ourselves. Our workshops have evolved into conferences: EarthSpirit Rising: A Midwest Conference on Ecology and Spirituality (1998 with David Abram, Rosemary Radford Ruether, David Orr, Dennis Banks, John Seed, Paula Gonzales and others); EarthSpirit Rising: A Conference on Ecology, Spirituality, and the Great Work (2001 co-organized with Cultivating Connections, including presenters such as Brian Swimme, Matthew Fox, Miriam MacGillis, John Seed, Paul Winter, and others); and Earth Spirit Rising: Earth Wisdom, Elder Wisdom: A Council of Earth Elders (2002 with Thomas Berry, Brooke Medicine Eagle, Miriam MacGillis, and Howard Hanger); EarthSpirit Rising: A Conference Celebrating Earth as Teacher (2004 with Diarmuid O'Murchu and Connie Barlow); and EarthSpirit Rising: A Conference on Ecology, Spirituality and Community (2005 with Matthew Fox, Winona LaDuke, Frances Moore Lappé, Miriam MacGillis, John Seed and Malidoma Somé).

All the while, cosmology—understanding our place in the universe—has continued to be the foundation for our work. We have continued to ask the questions: "Where do we come from? Why are we here? Where are we going?" These questions underlie everything that we do. In this book, we will consider how people today are answering these three primary questions of existence based upon what we now know or speculate about our universe. We choose to see the present as an incredible and exciting time for humanity. We are blessed in knowing that the old story no longer serves us as we develop a new story and a new mythology for our times.

Other questions we will continue to ask include: "How do we apply these questions to our everyday lives? How will a new cosmology affect our lives?" For, as Sun Bear used to say, "It isn't worth much if it doesn't grow corn." But that will be a topic for another book in the future.

INTRODUCTION

Homo sapiens evolved on the Earth about 2 million years ago. One of the striking characteristics of this new species was the development of reflective consciousness. With this capacity, humans began asking such questions as: Where do we come from? Why are we here? What is our meaning and purpose? Where are we going? What happens after death? Cosmologies were developed by humans in an attempt to answer these questions, as humans sought to better understand the world in which they lived.

Through thousands of years of evolving human consciousness, many different views of the Earth and universe developed. A fairly common view postulated the Earth to be a flat disk. The sun and moon circled the Earth, rising and setting each day. The stars filled the night sky. The "underworld" was located below the Earth. The existence of beings or entities more powerful than humans was another common belief. For some, these beings were beyond the sky. For others, they lived within the Earth. For many, they lived in both places. According to scientific research, the belief in a god or gods has genetically evolved within the human brain. There is a place within the human consciousness that orients humans to believe in a more powerful entity or entities. The pervasiveness of spirituality and religions throughout the human population, both historically and in our present day, strongly supports this finding.

Roman and Greek mythology are examples of Western thought that attempted to make sense of human existence. They spelled out very specific ways that humans related to the Earth and to the gods who transcended the Earth. For them, the gods were capable of coming onto the Earth to interact with its inhabitants. Celtic spirituality believed in a god that was much more immanent and existed within the Earth community. To have a relationship with this god meant having an integral relationship with the Earth community.

These cosmologies were developed by men and women trying to understand their world and the role of humans within it. Many metaphors for god and heaven were developed from such cosmologies. Having gained prominence over the past two thousand years, the predominant mythology in the Western world today comes from Christianity.

The following four men had an extensive influence on developing the myths and metaphors that underlie Christianity. Understanding how those myths were developed, helps us to understand the potential of creating new myths and metaphors.

HOW WE GOT HERE: THE DEVELOPMENT OF THE CHRISTIAN COSMOLOGY

ANCIENT GREEK PHILOSOPHIES : THE BASIS OF CHRISTIAN COSMOLOGY

PLATO

The Greek philosopher Plato (427–347 BCE), described God as:

- the eternal Being of absolute good, knowledge, and beauty;
- living above the domed sky in the world of the spirits and pure knowledge;
- God was Beautiful and simple in his own form;
- God did not change and was, in essence, Form – an unchanging reality beyond the world of our human senses.

The notion of a transcendent God was not a common belief in the Western world during Plato's time. The majority held that there were many gods, all intimately involved in the lives of the people. Relationships between the humans and the gods were totally interconnected. Yet, while Plato may have believed in the connection between these gods and the Earth, he also believed that there was an ultimate and perfect God that transcended the Earth and was quite removed from the interactions on the planet.

Plato reasoned that humans were drawn toward this perfection, but were shackled by their own imperfections:

- the soul was a fallen divinity, out of its element, and imprisoned within the human body, but capable of regaining its divine status by the purification of the reasoning powers of the mind;

- the body was part of the Earth and its basest materials;
- the body was on the same plane as that of the plants and animals;
- the intellect put us in connection with the divine by helping us to rise above the Earth. Humans were seen to be engaged in an ongoing struggle between the body and soul, matter and form;
- human interactions on the Earth kept us from knowing God and distracted us from our true purpose, which is to desire and pursue knowledge of God;
- humans were in constant struggle because they live in a body and the sensual pleasures of that body distracted them from philosophy, knowledge, goodness, and virtue, all of which connect us to God.

In the pursuit of God, Plato believed that we should not indulge in pleasures of eating, drinking, loving, or acquiring material things. He encouraged people to be entirely concerned with the soul, not with the body. He challenged them to seek good, virtue, philosophy, and knowledge and believed that throughout their lives, they should desire death in order to be reconnected with the Form in heaven.

ARISTOTLE
Aristotle (384–322 BCE) was another Greek philosopher who shaped human perceptions. In his theory:
- God was the Unmoved Mover;
- God was the ultimate cause of all things;
- God was pure being, pure thought;
- humans had the divine gift of intellect that could make them kin to God and a partaker in the divine nature;

- humans could become immortal and divine by purifying their intellect;
- humans could become divine by imitating the activity of God himself;
- existence was hierarchical whereby God, the Unmoved Mover, was on top;
- humans were above the plants and the animals because of the divine gift of intellect;
- the human soul, in essence, was part of the divine nature while the human body was part of the baser material world.

It is believed that the teachings of Plato and Aristotle would not have had much effect on the lives of the common people, were it not for Augustine and Aquinas. It was they who later translated Plato and Aristotle, and organized their teachings into a religious framework which touched most of the Western world.

DEVELOPING A WESTERN CHRISTIAN COSMOLOGY

AUGUSTINE

Augustine (354–430 CE), a Christian theologian, based much of his thought on Plato. Augustine, like Plato, believed there was one God who created everything out of nothing. God was the Good, was omnipotent and ruled over a hierarchy where he was on top, followed by angels, men, women, animals, plants, and minerals. God was the creator of time, yet was eternal, had no past, present, or future. **But unlike Plato's view, Augustine's God could intervene in the lives of humans through grace. God knew what each human was going to do**

and saw everything that humans did in time. Humans had free will, but through prayer could request God's help through grace.

Augustine lived for many years in what he later considered a state of sin. He regretted this period in his life, and that regret greatly influenced his philosophical beliefs. He believed that Adam and Eve were born in Paradise and would have lived happy, immortal lives if they had not sinned. He also believed that neither angels nor humans, when first created, had a complete picture of God. Not knowing the magnificence of living in the presence of God, they had free will to choose good or evil. Some angels who chose evil were cast into hell. Adam and Eve disobeyed and chose evil over good, bringing mortality and sin to all of their descendants. However, God gave humans a second chance and redeemed them through Jesus Christ, the Son of God, and second person of the Trinity. Augustine believed that we cannot save ourselves alone but, through our prayer and intercession, God can give us grace that helps lead us to him.

Like Plato, Augustine believed in the duality of the body and the soul. The soul was directly linked to the spirit world. The body, while capable of being tempted, was not evil at the time of Adam and Eve. Augustine believed they would have procreated in Paradise only for the purpose of reproducing children and not for pleasure, since the pleasures of the flesh and the Earth were viewed as pulling us away from God. After Adam and Eve sinned, humans became innately sinful and, driven by the sensual drives of the body, had a tendency to do evil. Only through grace and our own free will supported by this grace, could humans reject the pleasures of the senses in interaction with the Earth.

Souls were viewed as having one chance in this life, but they would continue to exist after death. Based upon their choices in life they were led either to heaven (a place above the stars, sun and moon) or hell (a place below the Earth) to remain there for eternity. If in heaven, they would see God as he is, and would not want to choose anything but heaven. Though man was seen as superior to woman, upon death, the souls of both men and women went to either heaven or hell. Death was sweet, as the soul was freed from the human body to experience the fullness of knowledge and of the spirit world. The sweetness of death brought the sweetness of eternal amazement, and of the All-Knowing.

THOMAS AQUINAS

Thomas Aquinas (1225–1274 CE) attempted to synthesize the beliefs of Augustine and the Greek philosophers. He saw God as neither matter nor form. God's essence was not the same essence as God's creation, though everything flowed from him. Therefore it was not possible for humans to know God.

Aquinas held to a hierarchy of creation with God at the pinnacle. However, we could see something of God in all creation, and all of creation was worthy of respect because it was of God. Unfortunately, the church de-emphasized this aspect of his belief while retaining his idea that the Earth is a testing ground to decide if a person would go to heaven or hell.

Aquinas saw all creatures as having souls. But only the human soul would continue to exist after death and was able to be united with God. Human nature was form and matter, body and soul. Unlike Plato and Augustine, Aquinas viewed death as an unnatural experience. It was natural for body and soul to stay together forever, but death was brought about by sin, and the punishment was separation of the soul from the body. At the end of time, there would be a resurrection when the body would be reunited with the soul. Humans – body and soul – would then experience eternal bliss in heaven or eternal damnation in hell, depending upon how they lived their lives on Earth.

IN SUMMARY
These philosophical beliefs have permeated Western Christian theology for more than two thousand years. Over the centuries they have been spelled out in ways that the common person could understand and follow. Eventually an exclusive Christian cosmology prevailed in the Western world. Within this cosmology, metaphors for God developed based on archaic human culture: King of Kings, Lord of Lords, Ruler, All Powerful One, Creator, Shepherd, Father, Supreme Being, Author of All Living Things, All Wise, All Merciful, All Holy, First Cause. These Christian metaphors reflect the hierarchical nature of the culture with God at the top followed by angels, then humans, then animals, plants, and minerals. At the top of the hierarchy God brought "the good people" to Him in heaven – the place of eternal peace, eternal happiness, eternal bliss, the place up above where humans could dwell in the presence of God forever.

The Christian cosmology provided believers with a deep sense of meaning and purpose. It provided an acceptance and understanding of death. It gave consolation in grief and motivation for action. It was a framework in which all the sorrows and joys of life could be understood. It also gave a rationale for why humans were on Earth. The ultimate goal of the Christian was to spend eternity in heaven with God. The Earth was seen as a testing ground for deserving heaven. The ability to resist the temptations and pleasures of the Earth proved one's worthiness.

One of the consequences of this belief was the devaluing of the Earth and a desire to dominate and control it. It is difficult to honor the planet or to consider respecting or preserving it as important when the afterlife is what matters; everything else is just buying time.

Broaching the question what would such men have thought had they lived today, what would their writings be like if they knew what we now know? Given our knowledge of the size and age of the universe, the Big Bang, the expansion of the universe, the relativity of time and space, the curvature of space, quantum theory, black holes, and micro level theories dealing with molecules, atoms, and DNA, there is little doubt they would have drawn some very different conclusions about God, life and death.

A NEW COSMOLOGY

During the last four hundred years, our knowledge of the universe has changed radically, and humans have begun to grasp a universe quite different from what was understood before that time. We now know the Earth is round and rotates around the sun, a medium-sized star among billions of stars, in a galaxy we call the Milky Way, which is one of a billion galaxies, each with billions of their own stars. Within the last fifty years, less than the span of one lifetime, knowledge of the universe has exploded. Every day, with the Hubbell Space Telescope and improved technologies, novel theories are presented about some aspect of our planet and our universe.

Acceptance of the new cosmology has begun to strip the old images of their power. However, there is a strong resistance since we feel secure with the old cosmology. The latest information is bombarding us rapidly, leaving little time to assimilate it and to develop innovative spiritual metaphors that give meaning to life. We need to develop new images of God, of life and of the afterlife. We need new spiritual images. We need images that integrate the knowledge of an expanding universe, a universe believed to be twelve – fourteen billion light years across. Grasping a universe of billions of galaxies with billions of stars has presented us with a formidable challenge. The mind simply cannot grasp the extent and size of such a gigantic universe.

Through the ages, in dealing with the mysteries of existence, the intellect has needed the support of imagination. This continues to be a critical necessity in the ongoing development of consciousness and the preservation of the planet. With our knowledge of the universe expanding at an exponential rate, the creative power of imagination must be unleashed, creating metaphors to carry the reality. Only through the combination of intellect and imagination can we bring the overwhelming realities of the universe to a harmonious state within our human consciousness.

What new metaphors can we develop from the new cosmology that has changed so rapidly over the past fifty years? Such words as Energy, Source, Spirit, The Force are the metaphors that connect more closely with the new cosmology.

With education no longer limited to a few elite males, it is possible for a much broader group of women and men to think and write about these issues. With mass communication it is possible for people to learn from many others and to develop their intellects beyond what was conceived previously. Today, the collective thoughts and speculations of many people about God, life and the afterlife are giving rise to concepts that are more relevant than those of the great philosophers of long ago.

The present view of the universe is so new and our knowledge is expanding so rapidly that any thoughts in this area are still rudimentary, albeit immensely creative. Most people would admit that we still know very little about the universe, but what we do know opens up a whole new horizon. This book encourages the expression of those spiritual metaphors and images based upon the new cosmology. It contains brilliant and ordinary thoughts. It is only a sampling, but one that might help readers analyze and deepen their own personal ideas about God, life and death. The hope here is that new metaphors will expand people's philosophies and theologies. Only in this way can we attempt to stay abreast of our expanding universe.

Since we are in the midst of creating a new cosmology, the views expressed here are broad and varied. Part of the excitement is that each of us has an opportunity to participate in the creation of the metaphors for the new cosmology. This creation is not restricted to just a few.

Because the images of God, life and the afterlife from

the old cosmology are so detrimental to our planet, new metaphors are essential for the survival of our planet our human species, and the many other species that share this home with us. The images expressed in this book may not express universal reality, but they do certainly have more truth and are more relevant than the metaphors developed by ancient cosmologies that no longer serve us.

In this book, I have chosen to focus on Western thought because it is most familiar to me, and I am sure, to most of the people who will read it. Thoughts from Eastern thinkers and from traditional peoples will help deepen the New Story, but are not the focus of this book.

The majority of articles are original writings or interviews obtained specifically for this book. A few pieces, which I thought were especially appropriate, have been taken from books and magazines. The contributions to this book represent an attempt to stimulate new answers to the age-old questions: Where do we come from? Why are we here? Where are we going?

PART ONE

Where Did We Come From?

The Embrace ©2001 by Marion C. Honors, CSJ

Where Did We Come From?

– BY –

Catherine Browning

Where do we come from?
Deliver us a line.
About supernovas and galaxies,
Empty space and time.
Do we come from the garden,
Do we come from the One,
Do we come from the fireball,
Or the generosity of the sun?
Weave a tale for us,
Spin a metaphor or two,
About the grandeur of our origins,
When the seamless web was new.

As I stand in the backyard in the darkness, stars glisten in the cool evening. My brain *knows* that those stars are light-years away, and yet my mind struggles to comprehend the reality of such distance. Standing there, I can comprehend a mile, or maybe even five. I can picture a distance from one place to another, and understand that distance if it is short enough. But when I consider more than a few miles, I can only comprehend by considering the length of time it will take to drive there. If 225 miles to Cleveland from Cincinnati is more than my mind can wrap around, what about eight light-minutes to the sun? Or four light-years to the closest star? A universe that is twelve billion light-years across?

Our human minds evolved in a tribal setting. In that setting, our species came to understand local change, simplistic theories of causality, and limited numbers. This is the way our minds work and how we understand events and things. Our brains are still too primitive to grasp the enormity of long distances and vast quantities. What is the chance, then, of our ability to comprehend a universe that is twelve billion light-years across?

Moreover, if we believe the universe was created by God, and that God must therefore encompass the universe, do we have the ability to grasp what God is, when we can not even comprehend a distance of a hundred miles, or the quantity of one billion, which reflects the number of stars in the Milky Way galaxy alone?

I can comprehend a man in a long white robe and white beard. This reflection of God the Father – especially father – makes sense to a mind that is able to deal with simple things.

Some might think it audacious to try to present an image of God. Our only resources to create an image of God are the limited words and concepts that have been developed over man's short years of existence.

With that disclaimer, words like Energy, Source, Nothingness, Force, and All-Nourishing Abyss convey thoughtful reflections of God for me. These are words I have heard others use that make some sense for me in describing God. It is hard to do, but it is important work, work that influences all else we do. So, we must at least try.

My own experience comes from being in the woods. Truly *being* there and listening. I speak and I am spoken to. When I experience the animals around me as I stand under a huge oak tree or sit quietly by the water, I am aware of, and know that I am part of the phenomenon we refer to as God. Having been raised in the culture of the twenty-first century America, where the dominant belief is that such phenomenon cannot be proved empirically and therefore must not exist, my well-trained habit of mind doubts that I am having an experience of God. Yet, at the same time, I cannot deny the divinity that surrounds me, and what my heart and my intuition know to be true. The patience and compassion that surround me in this setting allow me to be present without fear. Surprise and awe, burdened by my doubting mind, may best characterize my state. In this space, God is defined for me.

The writings that follow reflect images that others have of God. It takes courage to write about God, and humility in making the attempt, being aware that words and human perceptions limit the expression of insight. These writings are not offered as certain descriptions of who or what God is. They are offered as possibilities to help us reflect and broaden our own visions, as we create and expand our own images of God.

CHAPTER ONE

Where Did We Come From:
A Personal Perspective

Deconstructing God

– BY –

Miriam Therese MacGillis

Over the last thirty years, without any forethought, I have been deconstructing my images of God. My early mind and imagination were shaped in pre-Vatican II Catholicism and my images of God were ancient, clear, strong and beloved. Deconstructing God has been humbling.

Sandra Schneider has aptly described my sacred images of the Trinity as "two men and a bird." The central stained glass window in my parish church depicted a warm, elderly, white-haired man, a younger Jesus with a scepter and a beautiful dove above them. Interestingly enough, the two men are placing a crown on the head of Mary kneeling before them.

The image is indelible in my mind. This clarity and assurance about the nature of God gave form, assurance, meaning, and beauty to my life. I think this image also shaped my family, friends, schoolmates and the world of American Catholicism.

During Vatican II, without anyone realizing it, we began taking apart, dismantling, and examining all those images for what is beyond image. I know I have moved through this process. It has been very difficult. There were no guides. I just kept slowly dismantling my images of God. As a result, I do not have specific images. So now I have to try to imagine ways to approach the Ineffable Mystery, the Unknowable, the Holy One.

One of the images I have worked with is a pinpoint. The universe started with a very small area the size of a pea – according to Einstein. I picture that as a black dot in the middle of a white field. I can only sense what is behind the white field and the black dot. There is no way to know the Unknowable. I am content with that. I don't need anything more. The reason I have faith in this Mystery is that, on this side of the black dot, the universe is the testament to it. In other words, what I have come to understand as the universe, the Earth and all its relationships is miracle enough for me to trust what is behind the black dot. I do not need to know any more. That has opened a door of faith for me that is different from my earlier life.

In the past, my faith was based on the history of the Hebrew people, the life of Jesus and the historical church. This is how I perceived truth. My tradition of truth was the "inspired" story of the people, events, and circumstances recorded in the story of humanity after the Fall from grace. It is the story of hundreds of thousands of human beings living their lives while believing in a Divine being who guided their personal and collective destiny.

This is the legacy I have been given. Now I understand this story as the laying down of an inner spiritual legacy developed through lives of thousands of human beings who shaped their lives out of this story and created the insights, values and spiritual qualities as part of an ongoing developmental process of consciousness.

This is my Catholic legacy. It is the repository on which

I stand in the present moment, using its energy to keep myself going. This faith tradition has become a single seamless fabric behind my understanding of the universe, a gift upon which my consciousness can continue to expand. So it is a connection, an endowment, a legacy.

In my darker moments I fear that what is happening to our planet is so bad, so far gone that we won't recover. When I feel my grief and anger, when I let myself experience the pain of the world, it is this faith that sustains me. It enables me to keep going, to die to my small self and resurrect a new aspect of my deeper self. Crisis becomes a condition for opening me up. If I could not be faithful to my life's call through these dark times, I would abandon the whole thing. When I get tired or frustrated or overwhelmed by the feelings that it is too late, or that I ought to get on with another life and abandon this crazy path, it is my faith that keeps me going.

There is nothing else to do. It is a sense of a calling, of unfolding the meaning of one's life.

My relationship with the Mystery is in my prayer. I just imagine the field with the black dot and I'm in front of it. I say to it, "I believe, work through me, use me." I do believe the yearning of my heart is heard and accepted. I cannot be in this gorgeous universe and assume that it is random. This is not a possibility for me. I want to align myself with the good, with its purpose, rather than seek some sort of intervention or confirmation. Life is enough. This moment is enough. Sunlight, birdsong is enough.

We Are Creatures
of the Cosmos

– BY –

Diarmuid O'Murchu

We are creatures of the cosmos, sustained and nurtured within the living organism of planet Earth. We are creatures who belong, and from the web of our belonging we take our identity and our meaning. We belong to the whole of creation, carrying within our being the hydrogen and helium of the early universe, the carbon from exploded stars and, perhaps more than anything else, sunlight which is the critical ingredient of the food we eat everyday.

We are co-creative beings whose destiny is to work collaboratively with nature and with life. For most of our time on earth we have been faithful to that task; hence, the naming of *homo ergaster* (the human person, the worker) which the anthropologist Leakeys adopted in the 1970s to describe that stage of our evolution that dates back at least two million years.

I am not intimating that we are, or were, perfect, nor do I wish to glamorize the past. By nature, we are "raw in tooth and claw" (Tennyson). Often we don't get it right, but for most of our human story (possibly 6.5 million years according to the discoveries made in Chad in July

43

2002), we have related lovingly, meaningfully and collaboratively in terms of our planetary and cosmic mission. At our best, we are good at making the right connections.

At heart we are a creative species, the progeny of a co-
creative God. Deep in our hearts we know who we are
and we know where we have come from. Almost in spite
of ourselves, we reflect the grandeur and creativity of
our divine origination. And we have not done too badly
in our co-creative responsibilities. We have messed
things up at times, and we ourselves turn that into a
massive problem, whereas for our divine source, I suspect it is nothing much to worry about. After all, a God
of unconditional love can tolerate more than a little
foolishness from *homo sapiens*.

In a word, there is no major problem about the long-
term past, either for us or for the divine source of our
being. It has never been perfect, but it radiates evolutionary meaning, and I am in little doubt that the evolutionary process is fueled by a powerful divine energy. Our
problem today, as a human species, is our recent past,
not our distant past. What we have been up to for the
past ten thousand years (a mere second in evolutionary
terms) is the source of our deep alienation, pain, and
suffering, forcing us once more to ask fundamental
questions about the meaning of our existence.

We are living at the end of a patriarchal era in which
things have gone badly wrong for *homo sapiens*. We became over-attached to power games, trying to play God
and in the process alienated ourselves to levels we have
never known before. We have alienated ourselves from
each other, from the earth, from creation and even from

God. But there are indications that this crazy ten thousand year wave is beginning to ebb and with t hat flows the prospect of a better future.

Whether *homo sapiens*, as presently constituted, will see that future, is becoming doubtful by the day. But from our mass extinction, the co-creative life-force will beget a more developed (and hopefully, more benign) species, and the universe will continue to flower and flourish as God designed it to do.

??What Is God??

– BY –

Terri Maue

god is a wild woman, with stars in her hair and toes growing like roots down into the molten core of the earth

god is the ineffable stuff at the core of my being, the place I get to when I go farther in than I can go, more me than any name I could give myself

god is words coming from "nowhere," images popping into my head, the welling of yearning for peace, the pang that pierces my heart when I see my grandchild

god is the wailing at senseless death, the keening at thoughtless destruction

god is the grateful sprout, resting in sunlight after its exhausting push through the earth's wintry crust

god is the embryonic novel in 74 pages and three folders in my room and countless brain cells in my head

god is the muffled sounds of the world blanketed in snow

god is the snap of a twig in the fireplace

god is the dream of the beach and the shrill of the alarm clock at 5 a.m.

god is red-orange clouds filling the crater of Mt. Haleakala at sunrise god is lightning, thunder, and kids playing marbles on the sidewalk in front of the house in advance of the approaching storm

god is the shape of a letter and the firing of synapses that converts the shape to meaning in my mind

god is the wrinkles around my husband's eyes

god is moist chocolate cake with creamy vanilla frosting

god is cosmonauts and astronauts waving to each other in outer space

god is the burning rainforest

god is laughter, and why not

god is goodness, indefinable, yet I know it when I meet it – somehow and thank goodness for that

because that's how I know what god is.

Grounding and Connecting

Paul Knitter

C.G. Jung said somewhere that many of us, when we hit our mid-thirties, find that we have to bring our concept or image of God in for an overhaul. That certainly was the case for me, maybe even a little ahead of schedule. As I grew into adulthood, I found it more and more difficult to feel God, more and more awkward to talk to him. Slowly, I came to realize that my problems had to do with my image of God as a person, a super-person, all out there. This image just didn't work.

Fortunately for me, when I started to feel this breakdown, I had the job of studying and teaching theology – but not just traditional theology. Back in the 70s I was doing what nowadays is called comparative theology; I was exploring Christian experience and beliefs in conversation with other spiritual traditions. And this conversation spoke to my own personal problems.

As I look back now, I realize how freeing and affirming Karl Rahner's notion of grace was for me. Grace is not an admission ticket to heaven, Rahner taught us, but part of our very being; it's present from the first moment of creation, humanity's and the world's and it's not a divine seal of approval but, rather, the very life of God breathing in our own life. Then came Paul Tillich with his reminder that all our language about God – even the very word *God* is symbolic. So words like *person, Father, Trinity* should be taken seriously, but not literally. And we must be open to new words, new symbols – for the Mystery is always more than any word or image can capture.

What I encountered in other religions, especially those from Asia, seemed to connect with, fill, and expand the message I was hearing from Western theologians such as Rahner and Tillich. This was true in ideas such as the Hindu teaching that "Brahman (universal Spirit) is Atman (individual spirit)" and the Buddhist conviction that "Nirvana (the Ultimate) is samsara (the finite)," but even more so in the Zen meditational practices used to touch the reality within these images. I came to realize that what Rahner and Tillich were getting at is the non-duality of the Divine and us: God and the world are not two, but at the same time, they are not one. To experience God is to experience Other that is not other. And then came my dialogue with Native American spiritualities which told me that this Life was breathing in all life. The symbol that became real for me, thanks to this Native American vision but also thanks to my studies of ecology, was that the world is truly the Body of God, and I am part of that Body. I could feel that, sometimes even see it, in the quiet of a forest, or in the eyes of my dog.

So where has this process of overhauling my image of God brought me? Maybe that's the wrong question. I haven't arrived anywhere but I think I'm moving more meaningfully, more smoothly. The image or symbol of

God that seems to infuse the many symbols that speak to me is that of a personal Presence that grounds and connects. The Divine that I feel at Sunday liturgies (sometimes!) or that I sit with on my meditation cushion everyday is not a Person but a Presence. Yet it's a personal Presence because, from what I feel in my own life and what I see in nature and evolution, this Presence is up to something. What this Presence is up to is grounding and connecting – grounding and affirming each of us in an embrace that brings peace and strength, but also connecting and relating all of us and so calling and enabling us to live lives of compassion and love.

But there's one further ingredient to this image of the Divine that speaks to and moves me; it comes especially from my Christian roots and experience. For me, Jesus remains an inspiring and powerful embodiment (incarnation) and symbol (sacrament) of what it means to live a life grounded and connected in the divine Presence. Especially, he clarifies just what it means to be connected with others. From what I see in his own life and what I have seen in the way that life is lived in Christian Communities (especially in El Salvador), Jesus reminds me that the Divine Presence connects us, in a special, maybe even preferential way, with the victims of this world – that is, with those who have been taken advantage of, used or abused, exploited by the greed or selfishness of others. And today, we understand that to talk of victims is to talk of not only humans, but also of the very Earth Itself. Jesus (and other Jewish prophets) tell me that to feel the Presence is to feel connected with such victims. To know God is to do justice.

There is a symbol in my own Christian tradition that

helps me pray with this image of the Divine as Presence-that-grounds-and-connects. It is God as Spirit. Spirit is personal, but not a person. Spirit is a pervading presence that breathes in my spirit and so grounds me, but also a presence that connects me with other spirits. And because as a Christian I picture this Spirit as the Christ-Spirit I feel a special connection with and commitment to the victims of this Earth and to the victimized Earth.

To pray with this Spirit is not so much talking but being aware. Prayer for me is mainly sitting in silence and being aware. But I think the awareness has two aspects: it is an awareness in which I accept the overwhelming, peace-giving truth that I am grounded in this Spirit-Presence and that this Spirit breathes in me. But it is also an awareness in which I attend to how the Spirit may be calling me to connect with others. Prayer or meditation is a sitting in silence (a silence that is also possible during liturgies) in which I am aware of the Spirit and accept and attend to what the Spirit is doing in or as me.

Metaphors of Transparency as Well as Transcendence

– BY –

Michael Dowd

Growing up Roman Catholic, my earliest images of God were all literal. I understood God the Father as the All-Knowing, All-Powerful, All-Loving Creator of everything. Creation was a noun, an artifact, something made by God. I imagined Jesus, God's Only Son, as pictured in the Gospels: a baby in the manger, a gentle yet powerful man who told parables and loved sinners (like me), the sacrificial lamb crucified on the cross for my sins. I pictured the Holy Spirit sometimes as a dove, sometimes as tongues of fire, and sometimes as an invisible force or energy. How exactly the three-in-one business of the trinity worked I was not sure (I certainly didn't know how to see it in my mind's eye). My general sense of God, overall, was that he was a loving, if somewhat aloof and occasionally severe, being who resided off the planet and outside the universe.

Meanwhile, my *experience* of God occurred most powerfully in the natural world. I remember touching God while sleeping out atop a ridge overlooking the Hudson River, under a blazingly star-filled sky. God was right there with me, too, immersed in the cool waters of a frothy pool at the base of Bash Bish, a favorite water-fall. I often felt God's nurturing presence while sitting or walking slowly in a garden, enjoying the delicious smells and sounds and colors of summer.

During my later teenage years and into my early twenties, my religious orientation became that of a born-again, Bible believing, fundamentalist, Spirit-filled Pentecostal Christian. My images of God remained much the same, but the focus was now on Jesus, the risen Christ, as Lord of Lords and King of Kings, and on the experience of the Holy Spirit as evidenced through spiritual gifts such as speaking in tongues.

My images of God began to shift once again in college. After three years in the U.S. Army, at the age of twenty three, I enrolled in an Assemblies of God liberal arts school. On the first day of biology class, I was so outraged to learn that evolution would be part of the curriculum that I stormed out of the room, slamming the door. I complained to my roommate, "Satan obviously has a foothold in this school!" I soon came around, however (with a little help from my friends), and came to accept evolution as the way God created the world. Looking back, I can see now that this shift to an evolutionary worldview was the turning point for my eventual opening to an altogether new, equally meaningful, and more intimate and empowering relationship with God.

In the late 1980s my understanding and experience of the universe shifted profoundly, as I was introduced to the concept of cosmogenesis through the writings, audiotapes, and videotapes of Thomas Berry, Brian Swimme, and Miriam MacGillis. These three, along with Matthew Fox, Gene Marshall, Sallie McFague, and

Joanna Macy, not only helped me envision and interpret evolution as a spiritual, meaningful process. Collectively, they also helped me experience God, and life, in a more intimate, personal, and fully embodied way than I had ever experienced before. I cannot overstate the impact of the work of these brothers and sisters on my life.

From a spatial understanding of the universe, where the cosmos is understood as some *thing* separate from us (that we're gradually figuring out), or as some *place* (within which galaxies, planets, and living creatures exist): from this perspective traditional images of God make perfect sense. But from a time-developmental understanding of the universe – where the entire cosmos is understood as an autopoetic (self-organizing), developing process that has been expanding and becoming more complex, more aware, more cooperative and independent, and more intimate with itself over time – the need for new images of the divine is paramount. And with new images come transformed ways of experiencing God.

In the late 1980s I also began a quest to learn what images of the divine, of Mystery, may have existed for ancestral humans – for my ancestors. I came to imagine *homo habilis* walking upright, using stone tools, and experiencing the power, beauty, and majesty of nature. I imagined *homo erectus* domesticating fire, cooking, and perhaps beginning to develop early forms of spoken language. I imagined early *homo sapiens* further developing both tools and symbolic language, and beginning to tell stories about themselves and their indescribably awesome world. As I continued to imagine human language and culture becoming more complex over time, it just made sense that there would be a natural flow from animism, where every form of life has its own divine spirit, to the personification of Nature as the Great Goddess or Earth Mother, and then, with the advent of writing and the profound shift in consciousness that comes with literacy, to the personification of the Source of Nature as God the Father.

Moreover, it made sense to me that once we learned (only in this past century!) that the universe is expanding, evolving, and becoming more complex, aware and intimate with itself over time, and once we came to understand that we humans literally are the universe evolved to the extent that it can now begin to know and understand *itself*, we would, once again, need to revise our images of the divine.

So how do I picture God now? I imagine God as the Fecund Void out of which all things arise and into which all things return – the No-Thing-Ness, or Great Mystery, out of which the universe emerged fourteen billions of years ago and within which it is sustained and energized every moment. I see the entire universe as the Hand of God – the primary revelation of the divine – and God, the animating Life Force of the Cosmos, embodied or incarnate in matter itself. From this perspective, I can imagine God in any number of ways: as a father or a mother, as a lover or a friend, as a rock or an ocean – metaphors of transparency as well as transcendence. Each metaphor reveals a face of Mystery, an aspect of Reality. But, of course, no one metaphor or image can possibly show all the facets of the Source, Substance, Energy, and End of Everything – which is why a multitude of metaphors is to be welcomed.

Whether this understanding of the divine is ultimate

truth, I do not know. I don't think we *can* know. But I do know that this is a very useful, fruitful stance by which to engage with the world. It's an empowering way of seeing. That is, when I act as if this way of understanding the divine is true, I love the fruit of my life. This stance empowers me to love more deeply, broadly, and inclusively, and to live with more integrity and compassion than ever before. Moreover, I now experience God more intimately and personally than I ever have—not merely as a powerful, Supreme Being outside the universe, but as my larger self, my true nature, the cosmic embodiment of compassion.

Because I see the universe as the Hand of God, prayer, for me, is intimate communication between a cell in the body and the larger divine body of which it is a part. I still consider myself a disciple and follower of Jesus – indeed, I believe that my heart experience of God is more Christ-like than ever. Yet my images of the divine no longer emerge from a first-century cosmology. I can see how perfect my journey has been – how necessary for my own growth and development that I began with and moved through other understandings and experiences of God.

My bottom line is this: I trust the universe. And I can wholeheartedly say the same in a more familiar way: I have faith in God. Experiencing God as embodied and revealed in nature, and sensing the divine in everything, helps me make sense of the universe as I understand it through science. It serves me in my everyday life, empowers me to passionately pursue the work I know I am called to do, and helps me live a Christ-centered, Christ-like life. What more could I ask for?

Creator's Face Is Smooth and Unblemished

– BY –

Judith Boice, N.D., LAC

My understanding of Spirit transformed following my sister's sudden passing just shy of her forty-first birthday. I've since learned that a beloved's death is often a major re-evaluation time in people's lives. Some meet grief stoically and use the experience to reinforce their rigidity. For others the passage through grief offers an opportunity to re-evaluate the landscape of belief, spirituality and faith. I reflected on the maturation of my relationship with what I knew simply as "God" in my childhood. Even though I grew up in a Protestant church that eschewed images of divinity, I developed a profile of God that was a cross between the white-skinned, lean-limbed old man of the Sistine Chapel and a department-store Santa Claus. The old white man transformed into an androgynous being during the feminist awakening in my junior high school years. As a teenager I spent several summers backpacking in wilderness areas, and during those trips I came to know the power of the creator through the beauty of nature. The singular face of God shattered, and each element of creation became a fractal of that magnificent life force. The creator metamorphosed again when I was a college student becoming a purely feminine Goddess. I needed this womanly relationship with spirit to heal the centuries of patriarchy that have shaped contemporary Western religions. Years of contemplation and life in several spiritual communities once again softened the rigid gender designation, and my understanding of spirit resumed the diffuse, omnipresent divinity of my backpacking days. My work as a physician and acupuncturist further developed my experience of divine essence as I honed the ability to strengthen and move this godly life force or *chi*.

Throughout my spiritual journeying, my idea of *divinity* has remained rooted in the Earth and all of creation rather than a disembodied sky god lording over some celestial resort called heaven. I am most at home with ancient Tibetan traditions, my Shawnee family, and the spiritual roots of my Celtic ancestors who practiced the old ways of working with the underworld, the Goddess, and angelic beings. Divinity rests in the wilderness, the chapel, the garden, the bedroom, and my bones. When I am awake, Creator is alive in every aspect of my life.

My sister's death also uprooted my belief in a personal God. In retrospect I'm not sure how this concept of a cozy fairy godmother/father developed. Ruth's passing, in combination with another tragedy later that year, swept the remnants of a childhood God from my life. I suddenly understood that God does not stay up late at night worrying about the balance in my checking account. That is my job. Goddess is not plotting a career for me, repairing the roof, or inoculating my children against illness and tragedy. Creator had his/her own work and life to pursue: creating other worlds, playing golf, relaxing in a hot bath, whatever he/she wants to do.

When I recounted this realization to my Shawnee mentor, he nodded sagely. "Creator gave you life," he said, "and he/she, whatever you want to call it, gave you the ability to think and take care of yourself. That's your responsibility."

He paused for a moment, choosing his words carefully. "When I pray – and I do still pray – I ask for help in figuring something out. 'Creator, help me think through how to support my family. Help me figure out how to find a job.' You don't ask Creator to find the job for you, or give you the money. Life doesn't work that way. That would be insulting the intelligence Creator gifted you with. You pray as a capable person who needs help, not as a helpless being."

The Shawnee medicine man's words still guide me in my prayers. I continue to explore the essence of divinity. The shattering of old concepts has left a lot of uncharted territory, and I'm not terribly eager to replace one badly drawn map with another. Often I am uncomfortable in the new landscape; I like the security of a map. Even more, though, I am determined to see Divinity clearly. For now, Creator's face is as smooth and unblemished as Death's.

God Is an Active Principle of Love

– AN INTERVIEW WITH –

Brooke Medicine Eagle

What are your images of God?

Medicine Eagle: God is an odd word to deal with, in a sense, because the English language is a "thing" language, but God isn't a "thing." Names, especially in English, deaden and do not represent the vibrant, active principle of Love which is my experience of God/Goddess/AllThat Is. And if there is any image I have of God (for short), it is loving arms reaching, reaching with a magnificent heart toward us. It is light and exquisite and warm and loving and so very rich. That is my image of God. I believe that love is the essential energy in the universe. I sometimes think of love as the bonding process which applies to everything. For example, your own cells: They don't have to remain together. They are intelligent, active, independent and aware. The process through which they come together to form an Earth body for you is love. They choose to stay together, to bond together, in order to create a physical experience for you, and then they go on their way when that is finished. Anything which comes together basically does that through love and connection. Love on a truly magical level, I believe, vibrates everything into being, into material reality, then receives everything in loving arms when that process is finished.

What does prayer mean to you?

Medicine Eagle: The greatest teachings tell us that creation is already complete. All the possibilities are already present. What manifests for each of us personally we call forward with our heart, with our feeling, with our energy, with our thoughts, as they create our feelings. These vibrations we carry magnetize what becomes our reality, on an ongoing basis. That's why it's important to vibrate at the level of energy we want to manifest; otherwise we unconsciously manifest something else. Powerful prayer is the conscious creation within ourselves of that higher vibration, rather than a needy, whiny, begging for something from Creation from a negative place of fear, need, or greed. We vibrate what we create. The finest prayer I know is to thank Great Spirit for giving me what I choose to manifest, even before it arrives. That place of open-hearted receiving, of faith, of gratitude is the best prayer possible.

Images of God

– BY –

Avery Cleary

From the deepest place inside myself peering out through the longing of my soul I feel God. It was not always so. My earliest image of God was born out of a story that confounded my young mind. Where did this old man with a white beard live? How did he create everything? Was he related to Santa Claus? These questions would never be asked.

"Believe what you are told" went hand-in-hand with "do as you are told." Cross the line on either and there would be trouble. It didn't take much to intimidate a six-year-old. That image of God seemed to freeze in my mind.

God became a vague concept of some force outside myself. A force outside the world. A force that I would someday know if I was very good. It wasn't too clear what good meant, but it was all I had, so I concentrated on being good. "Do no harm" became my mantra. Easier said than done. I stepped away from God and didn't realize it.

I didn't know I was frozen until thirty years later when my six-year-old daughter asked me if God was real. "Yes," I answered cautiously.

"How do you know he is real?" I explained as best I

could. "Where was he anyway?" My explanation seemed to lack conviction, but at least I left out the part about him being an old man with a beard.

I was stunned when she said, "I don't believe he's an old man with a beard." I knew she hadn't picked that up from the Unitarian Sunday School because I had been one of her teachers. When I asked who thought that, she replied, "Lots of people. But it can't be true. Is it?"

Reassuring her God was much more than that, I tucked her in, saying good-night prayers. I reached to turn off the light and noticed an uncomfortable feeling in the pit of my stomach.

Who was God? How did I know it was real? How could I help my daughter feel God's love? Did I feel God's love?

It would be years before I could say, Yes, God is real. It would be years before I could say, I know God is real because I can feel God and you can too.

My appreciation and experience of God began to open up as I came to understand the depth and dimension of where I come from...where everything comes from.

Coming to understand my place in the unfolding of the universe shattered my perception of God, creating an opening in me for the new to emerge.

The experience of God that lives in me now is multi-dimensional: images, feelings, vibrations, fullness of being. My images of God no longer reside outside my being. They are in me and through me. I feel God in me and around me.

I can now take my grown-up daughter by the hand and show her God is real. In a flower...God; in the night sky...God; in a bird in flight...God; in a gesture of kindness...God; in her own reflection in the mirror...God.

God is mystery; God is life; God is all that is...all that was...and all that ever shall be.

You-niverse

– BY –

Marya Grathwohl, OSF

Last night I saw You for the first time. A fragment, 1 percent to be precise, of your magnificence was splayed across a classroom wall, electric light pouring You from a two-inch-square slide assembled from the patient eye of a telescopic camera. You(!) pouring into my being: universe and I looking into each other.

You slid out of Your vast and silent immensity, came singing and shimmering down around me. You quickened within me, awoke something old, long-slumbering, and visceral. I felt You, recognized You: my Source, my Ancestor, my Parent shining in the carbon of my bones, humming in the spiraling of my DNA, and dreams.

I slowly absorbed what I saw. Your undulating patterns of innumerable specks of light looked like the interior uterine wall or the complicated sun-and-shadow landscape of fertile garden soil.

The teacher was speaking, his words a drumbeat of meaning. "The smallest specks of light are clusters of ten to twelve galaxies. One cluster would be at least ten million light-years in diameter." With this drumming, even as You remained immediate, You leapt beyond every shore. Awe sucked breath from me, stung as tears in the whole of me.

Now, I am seeing You everywhere, the light within the light of each being You-niverse: stone of stone, flesh of flesh, wind of wind. Now I am dancing within the rhythm of You drumming, putting my feet down on soil of stars and pathways of immense abyss. What else does a person do upon meeting the Source and Mystery of All That Is?

God

– BY –

Gene Marshall

I am convinced that most people in our society, self-identified Christians as well as people who ignore or reject the Christian heritage, suffer an almost total confusion about the meaning of the word *God* as that word is used in the biblical writings. In our culture, "God" has become merely an idea, a way of giving meaning to our lives or a way of kidding ourselves about the meaning of our lives. But in biblical lore, God is not a way of giving meaning to our lives. God is not a belief or a hypothesis. God is not something you can believe in or disbelieve in. God is not a person. God is not an impersonal something. God is not any thing. God is not a being of any sort. God is not even a Supreme being. God is not an invention of the human imagination. All inventions of the human imagination are precisely not God, but idols to be avoided as objects of worship.

So what does, in biblical usage, the word *God* point to? It points to a reality, a reality experienced every day by human beings. What reality? What experience by human beings? Let me approach it this way: Every neighbor we encounter is being encountered in the master context of the overall flow of events. This neighbor has had an origin, is being sustained, is being limited, and will one day end. What reality has originated this neighbor? What reality is sustaining this neighbor? What reality is limiting this neighbor? What reality will one day end this neighbor's existence? We might call this reality by many names: Fate, Nature, Destiny, Mystery, the Ground of Being, the Enigmatic Power, the Void, the Fullness, the Infinite, the All-powerful, the All-Knowing, the Ever-Present. All these names are just names. Yet each of these names is an attempt to express some aspect of the human experience of that master context in which all experiences occur. Each of these names attempts to probe into the incomprehensible, yet ever present, Wholeness which surrounds or undergirds or encompasses the overall flow of events. This same Wholeness is, in the biblical heritage, being pointed to with the words "God," "Yahweh," "Almighty," "Lord."

"Wholeness" is just another human concept, but the Wholeness being pointed to by the biblical word "God" is not a human idea. This Wholeness is the reality behind all realities – the objectivity behind all objectivities, the subjectivity beneath all subjectivities. This wholeness does not give meaning to human life. Rather this Wholeness is precisely the Reality that unravels every meaning we attempt to give to human life. This wholeness is not the answer; it is the question. It is the experience of this Wholeness which raises in human consciousness the question, "What is the meaning of human life?" All answers to this question are given by human beings. God, in biblical lore, does not make sense of human life, rather God is that mysterious Otherness which awes us.

This awe-producing God explains nothing. This God is rather the Limiter of all explanations. This God is the mysterious surprising Overallness that upends all our attempts at meaning, all our paradigms, all our claims of scientific finality, all our programs of scientific research, all our philosophies of life, all our ethical systems, all our social laws, all our moralities, all our religious viewpoints. When, like a crashing tower, our life-meanings crumble and burn, we are experiencing that reality which the Bible names "God."

When some neighbor we value is given to us, we are experiencing God. When some neighbor we value is taken away from us, we are experiencing God. When some neighbor we hate or fear is taken away from us, we are experiencing God. When some neighbor we hate or fear is given to us, we are experiencing God. In every experience of every neighbor, we are experiencing God. What does all this mean? We don't know. God does not tell us. We are the creators of all our meaning.

One such creation of meaning is contained in biblical lore. The Bible asserts that the meaning of human life is to trust, celebrate, and obey this mysterious Wholeness that continually undermines all our attempts at human meaning.

Once such worship has begun, we can see that this mysterious Wholeness also supports us in our attempts to human meaning. Meaning is not forbidden to human beings; what is forbidden is any sort of absoluteness or finality in our life-meanings. Yet we do have relative certainties. We do realize that one explanation of an arena of human experience is better than another. We do realize that one way of operating works better than another.

These realizations indicate that we are sustained and supported by the overall Wholeness in our quests for meaning. Yet, at the same time, we are being limited in our meaning-quests. Again and again, we are cast into periods of fundamental questioning.

So in our quests for meaning, we experience ourselves as being both sustained and limited. The biblical heritage challenges us to experience ourselves as awesome freedom – the freedom to give meaning to our being sustained and limited. Then as we walk this path of meaning-giving freedom, we experience ourselves being sustained and limited in our attempts to give meaning to our being sustained and limited. All these experiences are our experiences of God.

"Loving God and Planet: An Essay on Eco-theology," *Realistic Living: A Journal on Ethics and Religion*, #22, June 1995.

A Prophet for the Earth

– BY –

Rich Heffern

In everyday terms, think for a moment about our sense of what "sacredness" or "holiness" has been, and of where these qualities can be found. Holiness and sacredness, of course, are attributes of relationship with the divine. In my own experience as a child, for example, the sanctuary of our parish church was presented as a sacred place, whereas that grove of sycamore trees down in the park, full of the magic play of light, shadow, aromas and refreshing breezes – in which all the neighborhood kids played and delighted, was not especially sacred to anyone of importance. The priest at our Sunday worship was on the inside track to holiness status, while my parents and neighbors were down the list. Even within my own person, there were thoughts that were holy and those (usually those associated with sex) that, in fact, were deemed unholy. The notion that the valiant, heroic struggle my parents fought to raise me properly was a truly holy one or even that my own awkward attempts to integrate an irrepressible sexuality honorably and sensibly into my life were an arena of blessing, were, let's face it, ideas akin to science fiction.

By overemphasizing one facet of who God is and where God can be found, Thomas Berry feels we have both gained and lost. What we have lost is the sense of God's pervasive presence within the creation, within the natural world around us. By establishing a covenant relationship with divinity, Berry says, we tend to diminish the relationship that exists with living world, with the plants and animals, with the mountains, the vast seas and the twinkling stars aloft. We cannot see these as evidence of divine activity.

Both ways of understanding God have benefits. Our relationship to nature depends on our understanding of how God is related to creation. Thus, our grave environmental predicament can be linked to our collective forgetting that, in Berry's words, "the trees, the birds, the various life-forms around us, are all voices awakening us to the deep mystery of life. The environmental predicament can also be linked to the deep feelings and spontaneities of existence that give us the fascination and healing we need."

In fact, our ability to imagine what God is like owes everything to the natural world around us. Why do we have such a wonderful idea of God? Why are the Old Testament psalms filled with such lively images for divine action in our midst? Because we have always lived on a planet that is chock full –every nook and cranny – with marvels and beauty, with mysteries, happy encounters and splendid landscapes. How could we picture God in our heads as an ever-fresh and creative daybreak, as a compassionate father, as a nurturing mother, a wonder-counselor, a luminous and caring enigma, if we had never experienced these qualities in the people, or the life, the animals, the shapes of the land and moods of the weather around us? What kind of God could we imagine if we lived on the bleak, sterile surface of the moon?

Excerpted from *Halfway Back From the Moon: Praying From Darkness to Dawn*, March/April 1993, #53.

The Sacred Is Immanent
in All Life

– AN INTERVIEW WITH –
Joanna Macy

What are your images of God, Spirit, Creator, Divine? What words, images or metaphors do you use to reflect this image?

Macy: There are a great many images since I have moved from the standard Christian view in my twenties, after my seminary studies. I felt some claustrophobia with an overly personalized center of all that is sacred. Now I see God in very immanent terms. I feel that the character of the spiritual experience of our era is to recognize afresh that the sacred is immanent in all life. There are images from that, largely natural images from running waters, deep rivers, blazing rising sun, with the great trees, great forest.

I agree with Rilke. I translated his *Book of Hours* and one of the things that drew me to it was his was turning from the image of God as the Great Father and King, sitting on a royal throne, to natural ecological images. He would say, for example, "When I lean over the chasm of myself I see you are a web, a hundred roots silently drinking." Or images of God as a great turning wheel. These seem appropriate to me and feel very Buddhist. From another of Rilke's poems, he would say, looking for God, "I see that You, God, are like a herd of luminous deer, and I am dark, I am the forest you are running through."

For the last century, poets and mystics have been moving more and more beyond an image of God on high to a sense of the sacred, all around us. That feels right to me. I imagine a great mind in which I can rest. It embraces and encompasses me and my little mind. So I would say that the images I turn to most are those that suggest the relationship of part to whole, of leaf to tree, of drop to ocean, of flower to garden, of grape to vineyard.

When you pray, do you have an image of God?

Macy: My prayer is very much like a centering into everfuller awareness, so it has a strong Buddhist tinge to it. My image of God would be like encompassing light or cradling darkness. There is a great figure in Mahayahna Buddhism called the Mother of all Buddhas. She is the perfection of wisdom. I sometimes imagine, when I meditate, that I'm sitting in her lap, that she is protecting my back and she is breathing through me. She represents the interconnectedness of all things, the deep ecology in which all beings are held, the web of life.

She Is Everywhere

– BY –

Meg Hanrahan

God is Life, is the Goddess. She is everywhere; inside and outside, and all around me. She greets me every day as the sun rises up from the hill behind my home. She walks with me, my feet upon her ground as I open the door and go to fill the birdfeeder. She flies upon the wings of cardinal, blue jay, dove, robin, mockingbird and sparrow, who come to feast on the seeds. And she is the seed. She is the seed, the soil, and the sprout pushing up through that dark fertility. She is the rain that makes the garden grow. She is the lettuce, the onions and the peas that nourish me. She is the green all around me, the bright color of the peony, and the fragrance that attracts the bee. The Goddess graces me with her image in these encounters in the natural world every day. Her presence is heard, seen, smelled, tasted, and touched in all these faces of nature. In natural environments, it is easy to witness God/Goddess/All That Is.

I come to know more of the personality of the Goddess in these encounters too, in the natural laws with which I become acquainted. Working in my garden, the lessons are plentiful, simple but profound. For instance,

I integrate on a deeper level simple truths, such as:
- That which we nurture and care for, grows.
- Sometimes we have to pull up one thing, to let another thing grow.
- Living things go through cycles.

That last one is big... The Goddess is always teaching me that living things go through cycles. The cycle of fertilization, gestation and birth, growth into fullness, decline, death, and rebirth is a common one. It's obvious that this is important because the Goddess illustrates this cycle in so many ways...In the life cycle of plants and animals, in the monthly waxing and waning of the moon, in the change of seasons and the wheel of the year – the sun's journey across the sky. In the ebb and flow of my own body rhythms, in the cycles of change I witness in my parents and children and friends, in the genesis of an idea into reality, fruition, and eventual change. Nature is always teaching me about the way to live my life as I immerse myself in the rhythms and the cycle of the earth. And as I come to live my life in those natural rhythms, I come to know the Goddess more. I come to know myself as a part of the Goddess; myself within her, she within me.

Though I focus my image toward the concept of the Goddess, the image encompasses god *and* goddess, male *and* female. The sexual aspects of nature provide structure/form to the dance of creation that we all participate in. Within myself, within humanity, within nature, I see the Goddess as male and female.

Other aspects of nature that inform my image of the goddess are diversity and abundance. Life is incredibly prolific in such a variety of ways; in every realm of nature toward which we look we see this to be true. Appreciating the realities of diversity and abundance in life, I appreciate many faces of the Goddess.

My own imagination and creativity reflect my image of God/Goddess too. In these, I find joy in living, purpose in work, and hope for the future. I hope to use this inspiration that comes from the Goddess to help to heal the world.

I find my image of the Goddess in that which I sense in the world around me...in the eternal drama that is life constantly being enacted, in the beauty and pain of that drama...in the abundant and diverse stories I witness in nature:

- The fast flutter of hummingbird wings
- The spider weaving its web
- The gentle ways of the deer
- The new crescent moon that sets at dusk in the western sky
- The waves of the ocean crashing onto shore
- Diamonds from the sun's light on freshly fallen snow
- Rustling leaves in a breeze
- A bright blue sky
- The owl calling my name
- The mountains that offer solitude, strength, and serenity to me

And on and on and on.

Immersing myself in nature, I see the image of the Goddess reflected at every turn – wherever and whenever I take the moment to appreciate Her presence – for she is everywhere and always around me.

Breathing In, Breathing Out: A Conversation With a Child About God

Kym Farmer

Feel that wind on your face, Danny. Doesn't it feel grand? Look at how it moves those leaves in the trees overhead. Can you see anything extra when the leaves are moved from one side to another? Look at the clouds, too – the wind scoots them along at different speeds and shreds some of them into different shapes. Let's watch some clouds change shapes... Close your eyes with me and let's see what we can smell on the wind... I smell some pine needles and some sweet-grass and a little citrus smell from the lemon tree over there. I feel a little moisture carried on the wind, too—probably from the creek down below. Hold up your pinwheel—the wind moves it, too. Turn it different directions and see what happens. The wind is moving the hairs on your arm, too, when you hold it, isn't it?

Can you see the wind? Not really. We can see the reactions from what the wind does. We can see the leaves move, sometimes even see the trees bend. We can watch the clouds scoot across the sky and the leaves scoot across the ground. We can smell more things when the wind is blowing, and we can feel things carried by the wind—water and dust and pollen and grasses. We can hear faraway sounds when the wind is blowing, and we can hear sound from the wind passing by—rustling in the trees and humming in the wires. But we can't really see the wind.

That's a lot how we know God. We don't really "see" God, because God doesn't have a shape. We can't really "hear" God, because God doesn't have a voice. But we know of God's presence because of our experiences. In that way, God is like the wind—all around us, affecting everything around us, bringing us gifts of surprise, and lots of information besides, and providing us with many opportunities for joy—every day and every moment, if we're ready to stop and notice.

The air surrounds us all the time, and can move and become wind at any moment. God is like that, too – everywhere present, within us and outside of us. Blow on your pinwheel – what happens? It moves just like it did when the wind blew it. In that same way, God's activity is outside us and inside us. God is like a presence, a force we can make use of once we know it. Can you feel God's presence around? Go and stand where you think God is... Where else? ... Where else? ...

How far out, then, do you think God extends? To the tops of the trees? To the clouds? To the sun? The stars? What effect do you think God might have on the sun? The stars? How far out into the night sky do you think God might go?

What do you think might keep those stars up in the sky? What do you think might keep our sun moving and our earth turning? The powers of God would have to be very strong indeed to do all that, don't you think? And also God's hopes would need to be strong, too—the longings of God's heart for this world of order and beauty we see all around us. There certainly must have been a lot of love there, for all the beauty around us to have come pouring out of the heart of God so many million years ago.

Walk over there. How did you do that? Did you tell your legs to move? And yet, somehow your body had the wisdom to accomplish that. Blink your eyes. How did you do that? Are you telling your heart to beat? Are you telling your lungs to breathe? Yet somehow you are carrying this wisdom within you. How do you think you learned this right away, as soon as you were born – even before that?

If God surrounds everything and fills up everything – the way air does, the way space does – then we know that God is a part of everything, in the same way that air and space are a part of our bodies in ways we can never separate. And if we know that before there was me or trees or Earth or sun or stars there was the thought and the desire to have it all come into being, then we know that God, this Divine Presence, must be a part of all things, that all things must have been longed for in the heart of God. So that makes me and the trees and the birds and the stars all part of one family – these are my brothers and sisters. These are you brothers and sisters.

And it also means that we are made of the same stuff. The water that is in these trees; the air that is in those clouds; the minerals that are in the rock; the bits of light that are in the stars; all these things are in me, because I am made from all of them. They're kind of like my great-great-great-great-grandparents.

Tomorrow, we're having a party to celebrate the birth of another of your grandparents, Grampa Lee. It's a way to let him know that we're glad he was born and that we love him, and that he has added so much joy to our lives. What kind of party do you think we should have to celebrate the birth of all these other grandparents of ours—around us, above us, within us? How can we use the breath we received from them in a celebration for them? Let's use your ideas for another celebration!

Intimacy of the Divine

– BY –

Peggy Logue

Another rain-soaked morning. Gray, mellow tones broken by greens holding glistening water drops surround my view. The grasses have more than risen their height and dropped their seeds in my new "no mow" zone. Trees have shot up new growth in soft holy green. The sight adjusts the sand in my early slumbering eyes.

The garden that was flat and lifeless is now delicately tall and full with exploding forms and colors. The house wren is chattering and flitting to her nest, which is alive with featherless creatures demanding to be fed. I am aware of the sacrament, of this holy moment of spring.

My eyes soft focus and I begin to go within allowing the boundary between myself and the life around me to dissolve. My intention is to be open and to receive. I allow my mind to rest and my spirit to awaken. I sink inside and reach a still point. I am aware that at a deeper level I am connected to all. In this state of at-oneness and openness I am at peace. In this state I experience the Divine.

My image of God is not an "other." It is only in experiencing sacramental moments that I can speak with any intimacy of the Divine. "God" is as life is. "God" is as the universe is. "God" is as the wolf is, as the child is, as the flower is, as I am. I experience "God" as I connect to what is in my present-moment awareness. Sacraments are moments of grace, reflected in the gifts of the universe. Sunrise, sunsets, seasons, elements, flowers, birds, life, death, rebirth are moments of sacrament, to name a few.

Our understanding has been: There is us, and there are others. This separateness creates arrogance in humanity. It allows isolated decisions to be made that do not enhance the Earth and all living beings. We now understand more and with new awareness the idea of potentiality. We are all. We are one. One universe. One song. Unfolding one story. There are no objects, just subjects. Creation anticipates harmony with all.

We, "thinking creation," are the universe understanding itself. We who write the story will listen to the voices of all beings and created life. We will hear the feminine voices, the native voices, the lessons of the wolf and the bear, the water and the air, the flowers and the trees. We will practice compassion. With our new awareness about our planet and the universe, we will redefine who we are and what our place is in this story. The God of the universe, the Ground of All Being is greater than we have imagined.

As we are more able to, "consider the heavens..." we are overwhelmed with the grandeur of the universe. My mind cannot grasp the number of stars, solar systems and galaxies.

How can we possibly define a "God" when we can hardly define our space in the universe?

As I close this writing the generous sun peeks through the trees calling a new horizon. The birds have awakened and sung their morning song and are busy feeding their young and gathering material for yet another nest. The chipmunk has scurried past me several times thinking she is so fast I couldn't possibly have seen her. Insects reflect sunlight; the frog croaks.

My image of "God" is present each moment I am aware: when I am listening and seeing and being fully present. In the intimate moments of connection with creation "God" is. "God" is the light, the dark. "God" is the wolf, the grizzly. "God" is the water, the air. "God" is the child, the parent. "God" is me... "God" is the present. "God" is all.

GOD IS.

CHAPTER TWO

Where Did We Come From:
A Universal Perspective

The Hidden Heart
of the Cosmos:
Humanity and the New Story

– BY –

Brian Swimme

Discussions concerning the vacuum sometimes point to the regions between the superclusters as the best approximation to a pure vacuum, and this is a reasonable way to proceed. Certainly matter and energy are extremely rare between clusters of galaxies. But the unfortunate consequence of speaking in these terms is to give the idea that the vacuum is far away, and this is simply not true. The vacuum is everywhere, and the place I want to refer to in discussing the vacuum is the space right in front of you.

In order to bring the idea home, cup your hands together, and reflect on what you are holding there. What are the contents cupped by your hands? First, in quantitative terms would be the molecules of air – the molecules of nitrogen, oxygen, carbon dioxide, and other trace gases. There would be many more than a billion trillion. If we imagine removing every one of these atoms we would be left holding extremely small particles such as neutrinos from the sun. In addition, there would be radiation energy in the form of invisible light, such as the photons from

the original flaring forth of the universe, or from An-
dromeda Galaxy and other sources. In order to get down
to nothingness we would have to remove not only all the
subatomic particles; we would also have to remove each
and every one of these invisible particles of light.

But now imagine we have somehow done this, so that in
your cupped hands there are no molecules left, and no particles, and no photons of light. All matter and radiation
have been removed. No things would be left, no objects, no
stuff, no items that could be counted or measured. What
would remain would be what we modern peoples refer to as
the "vacuum," or "emptiness," or "pure space."

Now for the news: Careful investigation of this vacuum by quantum physicists reveals the strange appearance
of elementary particles in this emptiness. Even where
there are no atoms, and no elementary particles, and no
protons, and no photons, suddenly elementary particles
will emerge. The particles simply foam into existence.

I understand how bizarre and far-fetched this might
sound for anyone learning it for the first time. But there
is simply no way to make this discovery "reasonable."
Most of us have Newtonian minds with a built-in preju-
dice that thinks of the vacuum as dead. If we insist that
only material is real and that the vacuum is dead and
inert, we will have to find some way to keep ourselves
ignorant of this deep discovery by the physicists: particles emerge from the "vacuum." They do not sneak in
from some hiding place when we are not looking. Nor
are they bits of light energy that have transformed into
protons. These elementary particles crop up out of the
vacuum itself – that is the simple and awesome discovery. I am asking you to contemplate a universe where,

somehow, being itself arises out of a field of "fecund emptiness."

The more carefully we study the universe, the stranger it gets. This emergence of particles out of a nonvisible field is not some unusual event taking place off in the regions between the superclusters of galaxies. This radical emergence takes place throughout the entire universe. The reason it took us so many millennia to discover this process is its subtlety. It takes place at a realm far more subtle than that which our eyes can detect. The usual process is for particles to erupt in pairs that will quickly interact and annihilate each other. Electrons and positrons, protons and anti-protons, all of these are flaring forth, and as quickly vanishing again. Such creative and destructive activity takes place everywhere and at all times throughout the universe.

The ground of the universe then is an empty fullness, a fecund nothingness. Even though this discovery may be difficult if not impossible to visualize, we can nevertheless speak a deeper truth regarding the ground state of the universe. First of all, it is not inert. The base of the universe is not a dead, bottom-of-the-barrel thing. The base of the universe seethes with creativity, so much so that physicists refer to the universe's ground state as "space-time foam."...

The true significance of the discovery of quantum vacuum is the new understanding it provides concerning the reality of the non-visible. I say *non*visible rather than *in*visible, for many things are "invisible" to us and yet are capable of being seen. Individual atoms are too small for the unassisted human eyesight to detect, but such atoms can be seen if they are magnified sufficiently.

The nonvisible, on the other hand, is that which can never be seen, because it is neither a material thing nor an energy constellation. In addition, the nonvisible world's nature differs so radically from the material world that it cannot even be pictured. It is both nonvisible and nonmaterial. Even so, it is profoundly real and profoundly powerful. The appropriation of the new cosmology depends upon an understanding of the reality and power of the nonvisible and nonmaterial realm.

In contemporary physics the nonvisible realm is not pictured or given any sort of geometric form. It is rather depicted mathematically and is referred to with such words as "quantum fields," "quantum potential," "false vacuum," "possibility waves," "universal wave function." For simplicity, I want to refer to this nonmaterial realm with a single phrase, and there are many possibilities to choose from.

I use "all-nourishing abyss" as a way of pointing to this mystery at the base of being. One advantage of this designation is its dual emphasis: the universe's generative potentiality is indicated with the words "all-nourishing," but the universe's power of infinite absorption is indicated with "abyss."

The universe emerges out of all-nourishing abyss not only fifteen billion years ago but in every moment. Each instant, protons and antiprotons are flashing out of, and are as suddenly absorbed back into, all-nourishing abyss. All-nourishing abyss, then, is not a thing, nor a collection of things, nor even, strictly speaking, a physical place, but rather a power that gives birth and that absorbs existence at a thing's annihilation.

The foundation reality of the universe is this unseen ocean of potentiality. If all the individual things of the universe were to evaporate, one would be left with an infinity of pure generative power.

Each particular thing is directly, and essential, grounded in all-nourishing abyss. Though we think of our bodies as dense and completely filling up the space they occupy, careful investigation of matter has shown that this is not the case. The volume of elementary particles is extremely small when compared to the volume of the atoms that they form. Thus, the essential nature of any atom is less material than it is "empty space." Even from this elementary perspective we can begin to appreciate that the root foundation of any thing or any being is not the matter out of which it is composed so much as the matter together with the power that gives rise to the matter.

All-nourishing abyss is acting ceaselessly throughout the universe. It is not possible to find any place in the universe that is outside this activity. Even in the darkest regions beyond the Great Wall of galaxies, even in the void between the super clusters, even in the gaps between the synapses of the neurons in the brain, there occurs an incessant foaming, a flashing flame, a shining-forth from and a dissolving-back-into.

The importance of the cosmological tradition is its power to awaken those deep convictions necessary for wisdom. Knowledge of all-nourishing abyss is the beginning of a process that reaches its fulfillment in direct taste. We think long and hard about such matters as a way of preparing ourselves for tasting and feeling the depths of a reality that was always present and yet so subtle it escaped us.

It may be that in the next millennium religious convictions will be awakened and established within the young primarily by such meaningful encounters with the mysteries of the universe, and only secondarily by the study of sacred Scriptures. The task of education then will focus on learning how to "read" the universe so that one might enter and inhabit the universe as a communion event.

Exerpted from *The Hidden Heart of the Cosmos: Humanity and the New Story* (Maryknoll, N.Y.: Orbis, 1996), pp. 91-93, 97, 100-101.

The Sense of God
Is a Sense of Mystery

– AN INTERVIEW WITH –

Thomas Berry

What are your images of God? What does God look like, feel like? How would you describe God?

Berry: The first thing is, God is beyond description. The sense of the Divine is a sense of mystery. As St. Thomas says, we have no direct experience of God. Our sense of God is as the source of all that is. So the Divine comes to us through the universe manifestation. That's why the universe was brought into being. It is a way in which the Divine shares himself. Goodness communicates itself and God wanted to communicate himself and could not make another deity, so God created the great diversity of things so that the perfection lacking to one thing will be supplied by the others. The whole universe together would participate in and manifest the Divine more than any single being. The Divine comes to us on all sides. We are surrounded, immersed in the Divine from the beginning of our existence. To try to consolidate the Divine in some single creative personality is one of the ways we can think of the Divine. For me, I can't think of the Divine as some single being isolated from everything else.

How do you pray?

Berry: Prayer is a communion with the deep reality of things. A person might say "deep reality." What does that mean? It means that which is not seen in itself but which is manifested in everything that is seen. We see the Divine, participate in the Divine and are immersed in the Divine constantly. This brings us to the question of our existence and why is there anything? It's because the Divine wishes to express itself in a fullness that cannot find a single expression. Therefore, the great diversity of things in their unity is where we find the Divine.

I don't pray in a sense that many people pray. I pray by a simple awareness of the deep mystery of things, the absorption and the wonder of the universe for the mind, the beauty for the imagination, and intimacy for the emotions. A child awakens to the Divine. The mind of a child is one of wonder and imagination of the world's beauty, of intimacy. It takes the universe to educate the child and it takes the universe to fulfill the child, and so the purpose of education is to bring these two together. That is why children are so intimate with other beings and why children need the natural world. Children like rabbits and squirrels and flowers and butterflies and the sea and the singing creatures and just the whole thing; a child is intimate with the whole universe. So with regard to prayer, the only way I can think of prayer is that it's a way of being with the ultimate existence that brings everything into fulfillment.

Reflections From
An Ecozoic Retreat

– BY –

Sr. Gail Worcelo, CP

DAY ONE

I have arrived at a retreat center on the East Coast and am beginning an eight-day silent retreat. I am going back and forth between texts that will serve as bedrock and guide for the upcoming days. Engaging in the ancient practice of *lectio divina* or sacred reading, I ponder the following words from the Old Testament text: "Wisdom reaches mightily from one end of the heavens to the other and she orders all things well."

At the same time I sit with an image of M100, a spiral galaxy that sits at a distance of sixty million light-years from us. This image was taken by the Hubble Telescope, whose powerful lenses probes into deep space and attempt to answer some of our oldest questions: Where do we come from? Are we alone in the universe? Who are we? And why are we here?

In the late evening I am able to locate M100 in the night sky. There are traces of God here. Feelings of deep reverence and awe arise within me. I wonder if M100 is still there or did it go out a few billion years ago in a supernova celebration? M100 deserves a better name!

Something like Luminosity, Radiance, God Bearer.

DAY TWO

I am accompanied on this retreat by the two Thomases – Thomas Merton and Thomas Berry, both of whom have been major influences in my life and who have, with intellectual precision, pondered the deep questions of our origins and source. It can be said that Merton looked at the questions, "From where did we come? And where are we going?" through the metaphorical lens of the microscope. Thomas Berry makes a subtle shift and asks the same questions through the lens of the telescope.

A few days before his death in Bangkok while visiting the huge carved statues at Polonnaruwa and after years of prayer in his Trappist monastery, Thomas Merton wrote, "The rock, all matter, all life is charged with Dharmakaya... everything is emptiness and everything is compassion." After years as a Passionist monk and scholar Thomas Berry says, "You can't think about the Divine without the universe, they are distinct but inseparable. The universe is the manifestation of the Divine in the phenomenal world."

DAY THREE

What happens once we move beyond the god of hearsay and enter into the God of experience? When we go into the country beyond words and beyond images? In our deep moments of spiritual revelation it all comes down to the fact that all is one, it is only one. We realize in the spiritual experience a profound singularity. Science supports that realization by showing us empirically that we live in a universe not a pluri-verse. The explosion in motion is one radiant being; conscious, whole, and undivided. I think we face a grand challenge, which is to manifest that wholeness as our humanity, to be human beings who are deeply undivided, living embodiments of an undivided self. This embrace of non-duality seems to be the herculean task of the Ecozoic Era. It is the call of the Spirit to be an expression of God, whole and undivided in this deeply divided world.

DAY FOUR

On this fourth day of retreat we gather in the chapel for the celebration of the Eucharist. I am moved by the simplicity of the elements of bread and wine, the hands raised in blessing, the starkness of the recited words:

"This is my body given for you. This is my blood poured out for you."

These words flow from an ancient twelve billion-year-text that tells the story of self-gift and grace. Supernovas, galaxies, plants, animals, carbon, lovers, women giving birth, martyrs of the faith, Jesus the Christ and all of us today, have spoken them.

We are the universe gathered in this moment celebrating its profound singularity. This explosion in motion is one radiant being; incarnate, conscious, Christic and undivided.

The basket of bread and cup of wine are passed around the chapel at communion and we all partake of this single energy event. I eat the bread and drink from the cup. There is actually no "I" doing this, only twelve billion years of holy celebration in joyful conviviality! The whole journey is this moment as it is the moment of the absolute future of Christ fulfillment radiating back to the present.

DAY FIVE

The paradox of the Divine in an evolving universe is that the glory of the Divine is both the radiant, complete and changeless ground of all that is, and the unceasing demand to manifest deeper and deeper expressions of wholeness and integration.

The universe itself manifests this mystery in its very structure. The curvature of space-time keeps the universe from collapsing, while the gravitational attraction holds all things together and enables the universe to blossom.

This compassionate curve is sufficiently closed to maintain coherence and at the same time sufficiently open to allow for continued creativity. There is something of the holy embrace of God here in the very structure of the universe itself. Changeless and changing!

It seems to me that the task of the Ecozoic Era is to manifest this paradox as our humanity. It is the challenge to be human beings who are living embodiments of the Divine, the perfect ground of all that is, in a world that is still deeply divided yet moving towards wholeness.

DAY SIX

This morning I am reflecting on a recent phone conversation with Thomas Berry in which he said, "We are opening into a new age of Mary." I recall a dream I had where the Black Madonna appeared to me in a field in her Christian manifestation as Our Lady of Czestochowa.

This image gives strength to my Polish roots and I have loved her all my life. She announces the Mystery manifesting its radiance in her flesh. She is Christ-Bearer, matter impregnated with Spirit. She is woman of grace, accepting her own body as the chalice of the Spirit.

There is a beautiful icon of Our Lady of Czestochowa in the monastery chapel. I sit before her in an open gesture of prayer. This Black Madonna has long been worshipped as "The One Who Leads the Way." The radiance that shines through her darkness is magnetic. She teaches me how to love my body and how to bring forth the Mystery embodied in my own flesh for the life of the world.

Wherever the Black Madonna lives there is deep silence, there is solitude. I find myself going to places filled with her presence. Praying before her in this still, dark chapel I hear her say, "All matter is holy. Divinity is revealed in every being as well as within the comprehensive unity of the whole."

DAY SEVEN

The person directing my retreat gives me a koan to break open when she says, "Be still in the monastery you are." The monastery I am is the vastness of the universe itself rooted in the Evolving Stillpoint.

What are some new images of the Divine for me? God is the dark matter between galaxies, the expansion of space, the space into which it expands, and the eternal evolutionary stillpoint. God is the curvature of space, the Trinitarian principles of differentiation, interiority and communion. God is the love bliss of gravity, the magnetic attraction of absolute love that asks for nothing less than everything from us. God is a raging fire burning wildly and consuming all. God is the fire within the fire of all things. God is beyond all that I have just said!

DAY EIGHT

If Teresa of Avila wrote about the interior castle as a metaphor for the spiritual life, I want to consider

Cosmogenesis as the modern-day metaphor for our journey God-ward. In this way the spiritual life can be understood as an evolutionary sequence of irreversible transformations of the soul. Spirit and matter evolve simultaneously and each generation becomes a further phase change of the initial radiance of the Divine at the beginning of time.

Where are we going? We have already arrived, all of us, and we will be forever evolving. The unborn future is already pressing upon us as faint whisperings, which say, "All things are bonded together in inseparable and everlasting unity."

It Doesn't Help Me to Think There Is Something Outside

– BY –

John Seed

In my life there's nothing helpful about seeing anything outside the universe that is creating it. The universe itself is this single integrated activity. It doesn't help to think there is anything outside that is causing that to happen. Now, it could be, of course, but for me all of the miraculous things that have been attributed to any God are completely included within the universe.

The universe appeared from nothing and created itself in that way. This satisfies all my hunger for the miraculous. I don't need a bigger story than that.

The Organizing
and Animating Intelligence

– BY –

Bill Cahalan

I see the pervasive, intelligent activity, which is inherent in the dance of matter and energy constituting the universe, as equivalent to, or at least as a significant manifestation of Spirit, Divine Presence, or God. Various theologies or beliefs about the nature of ultimate reality are possible here. Personally, I lean toward Arthur Green's statement, in an article proposing a new form of Jewish mysticism, that this "new story" provided by the sciences suggests a relationship between the universe and God which is less that of creation to creator than that of surface to deep structure. But this sense of immanent divinity also does not contradict the belief by others in a creator who transcends the creation as well as dwells intimately within it.

GOD?

– BY –

T. Jack Heckelman

I've been having increasing problems with the word *God*,
as it does not seem to me to be big enough to encompass
the cosmic consciousness which created the universe
and has guided its evolution. I think I have been able to
move beyond the childhood image of a bearded old man
on a throne, or Michaelangelo's magnificent vision in
the Sistine Chapel. For me, our culture has created a too
anthropomorphic a view of *God*.

This human-centered image of God is all-pervasive,
whether it is "his" watching over every human action,
our prayers for "his" personal intervention in our affairs,
or even our continuing debate over gender – is it "God
he" or "God she?" We automatically assume his/her
unique connection to humanity and to planet Earth.

I have to admit I don't have an adequate alternative
word. With Thomas Berry I agree we need a new vocabu-
lary to fully describe the "new story" of the fifteen billion -year evolution of the universe, and the consciousness which pervades it all. Recently the term "Ultimate
Mystery" has been a useful term, but as I have become
imbued with the universe Story I have used the term

"Cosmic Consciousness" to start to describe how I feel.

All my life I've been searching not only for new meanings, but also for a "universal religion" which would express those meanings for me in the largest sense. I am a Unitarian Universalist, and now somewhat whimsically refer to myself as a "universe-alist."

The best understanding I have developed so far is that of a "universal cosmic consciousness" that created the conditions leading to the Big Bang or the "flaring forth," as the beginning of our universe is now called, including all the potentialities of subsequent evolution. That consciousness pervades all that has evolved, and lives in all beings, including human, which are part of the current stage of evolution of planet Earth. That consciousness has guided the evolution of the universe, from the initial formation of the fundamental laws and particles through every stage, not necessarily predestined or preordained, but with a general "plan" (again no adequate word exists) of direction. At certain steps of the process, such as the evolution of life, quantum leaps which we can only call "miracles or "moments of grace" have taken place.

Now, in our present stage of understanding, with free will present in humans, the directions of evolution are in question, and we humans have a pivotal role and responsibility in determining that direction. May the cosmic consciousness in all of us lead us in the right direction – toward an Ecozoic Era where we live in harmony with Planet Earth, our home in the universe.

Divine Mystery, Giving Mystery, the All-embracing One

– AN INTERVIEW WITH –

Virginia Froehle

Who is God?

Froehle: God has grown more expansive, more abstract and more intimate for me. The earth, the whole universe, all that is, is an expression of the Creative Mystery. I do believe that this Mystery is more than the universe, just as the whole can be more than the sum of its parts, as we learn from quantum physics.

Do you have any images of God?

Froehle: It is impossible to speak of God without using images of some kind. Most people think of images as visual ones. To understand that we have many images that are not visual, let me offer you the probability that you can walk in total darkness up and down a stairway in your home without any mental images of the inches or feet you are climbing. You may be thinking of what happened yesterday. Your body has a sensed image of the distances and carries you safely. We also have images of

God – of relationship, of gender, of place – without any pictures in our minds.

The images that I have grown to use are more abstract, ones like the Divine Mystery, the All-Embracing One, the Giving Mystery, the All-Loving One and Wisdom. Although I have many more, these are some of the ones I use the most when I write.

When I pray, however, it is more to the Spirit who is within me, within you and within the whole universe. In the Spirit, I am connected to all things. As a part of the Creative Mystery, an expression of it, the Spirit of God is totally within me just as within you. In holograms, the whole is in each part. So the relationship with the Spirit is deeply intimate for me and for everyone who chooses to be open to It.

Do you have any visual images of God?

Froehle: I don't think so, though all the images we have ever had remain someplace in our unconscious. While we do use images in prayer and in speaking about God, it is important to know that an image is not God. Images change. What I'm saying about the Sacred now wouldn't have come from me a number of years ago. And who knows what I will be saying ten years from now, if I am still living.

God to Goddess

– BY –

Janet Schenk

As a youth
God was all, all, all –
  all present,
  all powerful,
  all knowing,
  all loving.
Puppet was I
  in his hands.
Meditation – mental prayer –
  was blank, a joke.

A shock one day!
  Anger sizzled,
    puppet strings snapped.
  Instead of crumpling,
    limp to the floor,
  I stood tall,
    and looked God in the eye,
    "Things must change,"
    I said with a glare.

A different relationship
  then ensued.
Growth occurred
  trudging but constant.
We talked together
  God and I;
 . *we argued, skipped, and worked,*
  until I faced
    a high solid wall.

God disappeared!
  I searched and searched.
I was ridiculed, thwarted –
  Wow, what pain,
  what torture
  to change so drastically.

Then like a butterfly
  I broke out
    free and beautiful.
  Strength was mine;
    I would depend on me!
  I flourished so,
    like never before.
A brand new life,
  on with human assistance.
Even so loneliness was embracing,
  but it had been before –
  There was a void.
    an aching void.
  What would fill it?
    Where to find.

I searched and wrote,
read and shared.
Out of this
gradually emerged

Goddess! – a new life –
life-giver, nurturer,
protector, venturer
revenger, consoler.
Feminist like myself!
I walked, ran, struggled,
wept, laughed, rested
with this power within, without.
Sometimes loud and clear;
Sometimes silent;
Sometimes positive;
Sometimes confronting.
She is here!

A Universal Process

Edgar Mitchell

What is your image of Creator, God, Spirit, Divine?

Mitchell: We live in a self-organizing, intelligent, creative, learning, trial and error, interactive, participatory, evolutionary system. And that intelligent creative aspect of it is what we call God.

What kind of images or metaphors do you have?

Mitchell: I am a scientist, but one who has looked at the subjective experience in particular the transcendental states of consciousness that have led to the mystical experience that led to religion. The mystical experience seems to be the root for all religion and it's the same in every culture. Let's call that the esoteric experience. When you attempt to explain it and put it into words, then it becomes the esoteric or the cultural expression.

The esoteric is the same the world over. The cultural expression (esoteric) is different the world over because it's culturally based in their language, their belief system and their experience. Since the esoteric is common the world over, it is something science can and should study. And that is what I've been doing; trying to understand consciousness from the point of view of science and studying the strange, wonderfully mysterious conditions we call subjective experience. Particularly I am looking at the so-called (although I don't like this word) "paranormal" expressions in that consciousness. There is overwhelming support for the validity of these expressions, but an explanation has not been available until now. It looks as if this all comes out of the quantum nature of matter, particularly biomatter. These wonderfully mysterious, exotic experiences that go with religion and the paranormal seem to be fully rooted in the quantum connectedness of nature itself. Many mainstream scientists will dispute that, but I think they're wrong and I think in due course that point of view will prevail.

In light of all this, what is your image of God or whatever that is?

Mitchell: I don't see God as an anthropomorphic being, a grandfather figure. That's old hat. That's just ancient stuff. Hardly anybody who has studied the issue really thinks that way anymore. We are in a universal process and we're even getting to the point of being able, very shortly I believe, to create a quantum cosmology that shows exactly how this came to be.

The Empowering Intimacy of the All-Nourishing Abyss

– BY –

Mary Coelho

As we ponder the ancient story of the evolutionary universe, it becomes evident that its unfolding and complexity derive from inner, generative dynamics and ordering powers. The whole process from the minutest events in the atomic nucleus to grand galactic interactions cannot have been guided by a power extrinsic to the physical world. There is no outside, as space is intrinsic to the unfolding whole.

We know there is a creative, organizing power permeating the entire world because the astounding diversity and complexity of the universe could not have come into being by random interactions, even over 13.7 billion years. The chances are negligible that a galactic structure will evolve randomly within one billion years, the approximate time from the beginning of the universe until it formed. With one hundred billion years, the chances are still negligible. The formation of amino acids, the building-blocks of proteins, provides another example. For atoms to bounce together haphazardly to form a single molecule of amino acid would require more time than has existed since the beginning, even a hundred times more than 13.7 billion years.

Human identity is informed by this knowledge coming from this implication of the discovery that we live in
an evolutionary universe because the creative, formative
dynamics are the same at every point in the universe.
This is the cosmogenetic principle. "The same dynamics
that formed the mountains and continents are the dynamics that eventuated into humans."[1] We will use the
phrase All-Nourishing Abyss, a phrase proposed by Brian Swimme, to denote this immanent, mysterious generative, formative order, except when quoting or referring to the work of people who use the word *God*.

We may wonder how these dynamics permeate us
when matter so solid and our bodies and the natural
world behave in a largely predictable manner. Physicists
tell us that if you take a simple atom and make it as large
as Yankee Stadium, it would consist almost entirely of
empty space. The center of the atom, the nucleus, would
be smaller than a baseball sitting out in center field. The
outer parts of the atom would be tiny gnats buzzing
about at an altitude higher than any pop fly a slugger
could hit. "And between the baseball and the gnats?
Nothingness. All empty."[2] It is not really empty, but only
empty of things we can measure and detect. David Bohm
asserts the "empty space" is full rather than empty. The
nonvisible, creative, formative powers are placed in this
realm. Werner Heisenberg has argued that the emptiness is equivalent to what the Buddhist call *sunyata*,
prior to anything that "is." Religious traditions have
also spoken of a No-thing-ness. We can thus imagine the
plenary emptiness that permeates us. "You are more fecund emptiness than created particles."[3]

Although we cannot facilely collapse together what

some scientists are now saying about this realm of emptiness with the ideas of God in the contemplative tradition, we believe that there is an important congruence of insight with regard to the supreme intimacy of that realm with the person. Jan van Ruusbroec declared that, by their very nature, people have an essential unity with God. He called it the "Imageless Ground." "This is the nobility which we naturally possess in the essential unity of our spirit, which is at this level naturally united with God (*Spiritual Espousals*, p. 118)." He wrote: "To comprehend and understand God as he is in himself, above and beyond all likeness, is to be God with God, without intermediary (Ruusbroec, Preface, p. xiii)."

St. Teresa of Avila, the sixteenth-century Carmelite nun, offers several images in her classic book *The Interior Castle*, which suggest a dimension of the person is in some manner inseparable from God and that we may know this in contemplation:

> In the spiritual marriage the union is like what we have when rain falls from the sky into a river or fount; all is water, for the rain that fell from heaven cannot be divided or separated from the water of the river. Or it is like what we have when a little stream enters the sea, there is no means of separating the two. Or, like the bright light entering a room through two different windows; although the streams of light are separate when entering the room, they become one.[4]

These images seem to indicate that in her experience the essence of the person is of the very same nature as

God (an ontological or substantial union). Teresa refers to the union as occurring "in the deepest center of the soul which must be where God himself dwells."[5] She once wrote of her experience of "mystical marriage," a type of unitive contemplation: "In my opinion there is no need of any door for Him to enter."[6] If there is no need of a door, God must already be in some manner integral to the person.

Friedrich von Hügel (1852–1925), the great modernist Catholic theologian, believed we should reject any absolute qualitative difference between the soul's deepest possibilities and ideas of God. Lawrence Kushner (1943 –) writes, drawing on the Hebrew Bible and the rabbinical tradition, in the *River of Light* :

> There is a place from which all places can be seen.
> And time from which all time might be beheld. This
> place is in us and was once shown to us even as it is
> still within us to this day... This place precedes life
> in this world and yet exists simultaneously with it.
> Its knowledge remains sealed in us.[7]

Some writers, both in the Christian and Hebrew traditions, have been at pains to maintain a distinction between the person and God in order to be faithful to the biblical distinction between the Creator and created. But, in Christianity at least, this distinction is severely challenged and in fact contradicted by the radical Christian assertion that Jesus of Nazareth was fully divine and fully human. Tragically this insight has too often been limited to Jesus but in the light of the new story and the contemplative tradition, any of us may potentially realize this unity within our person.

We no longer need to be angry at a Father who fails to come to us. We can instead trust the creative process that has perdured for 13.7 billion years and prepare ourselves to join in it as fully as possible. Brian Swimme defines enlightenment as "awareness of the depth of our belonging." The new story offers us such enlightenment. We can embrace with joy the depth of out participation in an ongoing process that has created such beauty, such diversity and such grandeur. May we be moved, as individuals with free choice, to give ourselves to the great creative process in which we are so deeply embedded.

---

1 Swimme, Brian and Thomas Berry. *The Universe Story: From the Primordial Flaring Forth to the Ecozoic Era—A Celebration of the Unfolding of the Cosmos* (San Francisco: HarperSanFrancisco, 1994), p. 66.

2 Swimme, Brian. *The Universe Is a Green Dragon: A Cosmic Creation Story* (Sante Fe, NM.: Bear and Company, 1984), p. 37.

3 Swimme, Brian. *The Universe Is a Green Dragon*, p. 37.

4 Theresa of Avila, *The Interior Castle*, VII, ii, 4.

5 *The Interior Castle*, VII, 2.

6 *The Interior Castle*, VII, ii, 3.

7 Kushner, Laurence, *The River of Light: Spirituality, Judaism, Consciousness* (Wookstock, Vt.: Jewish Lights, 1981), p. 84 .

8 Wilmont, Lawrence F., *Whitehead and God: Prolegomena to Tehological Reconstruction* (Watherloo, Ontario: Wilfrid Laurier University Press, 1995), p. 4.

Hymn to the Sacred Body of the Universe

– BY –

Drew Dellinger

Let's meet
at the confluence
where you flow into me
and one breath
swirls between our lungs

for one instant
to dwell in the presence of the galaxies
for one instant
to live in the truth of the heart
the poet says this entire traveling cosmos is
"the secret one slowly growing a body"

two eagles are mating—
clasping each other's claws
and turning cartwheels in the sky
grasses are blooming
grandfathers dying
consciousness blinking on and off
all of this is happening at once
all of this, vibrating into existence

out of nothingness

every particle
foaming into existence
transcribing the ineffable

arising and passing away
arising and passing away
arising and passing away
23 trillion times per second—
when Buddha saw that,
he smiled.

16 million tons of rain are falling every second
on the planet
an ocean
perpetually falling
and every drop is your body
every motion, every feather, every thought
is your body
time
is your body
and the infinite
curled inside like
invisible rainbows folded into light

every word of every tongue is love
telling a story to her own ears

let our lives be incense
burning like a hymn to the sacred
body of the universe

my religion is rain
my religion is stone
my religion reveals itself to me in
sweaty epiphanies

every creature, every species is your body
so yes I protest
and I just say no
to the I.M.F., World Bank and W.T.O.
because that primate species that went extinct
last week
was your body

10 million people are dreaming
that they're flying
junipers and violets are blossoming
stars exploding and being born
god is having déjà vu
I am one elaborate crush
we cry petals
as the void is singing

you are the dark
that holds the stars
in intimate distance
and spun the whirling, whirling,
world
into existence

let's meet

at the confluence

*where you flow into me
and one breath
swirls between our lungs*

Dimensional Cosmology

– BY –
Duane Elgin

A subtle Life-force infuses, sustains, and unifies our cosmos. The wholeness of our reality is so complete that we are not separate from "God" or "Nirvana" or "Brahman" or "Tao" or the countless other names given to the unnamable presence that pervades the undivided universe. We don't have to do anything to become a part of the wholeness of the reality—we are already completely at one with it. We are beings that the universe inhabits as much as we are beings that inhabit the universe. An appreciation of the unity of existence is not an experience to be created; rather it is an always-manifesting condition of our existence waiting to be welcomed into awareness...

The perennial wisdom agrees that the nature of the Meta-universe is ultimately beyond description. Still, attempts have been made to describe its paradoxical qualities, for example, by Zen Buddhists who have penetrated deeply into the nature of reality through meditation.[5] Interestingly, their descriptions are surprisingly similar to those of Western physicists of the late 1800s, who were trying to articulate the nature of what was then called the ether, or the underlying structure of material reality.[2] Following are some of the key properties of the Meta-universe that seem congruent with insights from both East and West:

- **Profoundly creative**—Compared with that of humans, who do not know how to create a single flower or cubic inch of space, the creative power of the Meta-universe is of incomprehensible magnitude, depth, and subtlety.

- **Everywhere present**—The clear, unbounded Life-energy of the Meta-universe is present in all material forms as well as in seemingly empty space.

- **Nonobstructing**—The Meta-universe is a living presence out of which all things emerge, but it is not itself filled in or limited by these things. Not only are all things in it, it is in all things—mutual interpenetration without obstruction.

- **Utterly impartial**—The Meta-universe allows all things to be exactly what they are without interference. We have immense freedom to create either suffering or joy.

- **Ultimately ungraspable**—The power and reach of the Meta-universe is so vast that it cannot be grasped by our thinking mind. As the source of our physical existence, thinking process, and reflective consciousness, it is beyond the ability of our limited faculties to capture and concretize conceptually.

- **Beyond form**—The Meta-universe is the source of both material forms and the space-time within which those forms present themselves. Being the source of the context of all forms, the Meta-universe transcends the world of form.

- **No objective measurement**—It is impossible to prove the existence of the Meta-universe through objective measurements, since it is the source and basis for all objective phenomena. The Meta-universe is of infinite dimensionality, so we cannot limit it to the few dimensions that we inhabit so as to measure "it."

- **More than nothing**—Because Meta-universe can generate an entire cosmos with billions of galactic systems and life-forms, it is much more than simple emptiness.

- **Immanent**—The Meta-universe is not separate from us, nor is it other than the "ordinary" reality continuously present around us.

- **Transcendent**—The Meta-universe is of the infinite dimensionality and reaches far beyond our dimensionally bounded cosmos.

- **Compassionate**—To experience the subtle and refined resonance of the Meta-universe is to experience unconditional love. Boundless compassion is the essence of the underlying generative ground.

1. John Welwood, "On Psychological Space," *Journal of Transpersonal Psychology*, Vol. 9., No. 2 (1977), p. 106.
2. Although the famous Michelson and Morley experiment in physics disproved the existence of ether as a static and external ocean that matter could push against, there are a number of attributes of ether theory that are highly dynamic and strikingly similar to the all-sustaining "void" of Eastern spiritual traditions. See, for example, the Duke of Argyll, *The Unity of Nature* (New York: John Alden, 1884), p. 18; and David Heagle, *Do the Dead Still Live?* (Philadelphia: Judson, 1920), pp. 43–44.

Excerpted from *Awakening Earth: Exploring the Evaluation of Human Culture and Consciousness* (New York: William Morrow, 1993), pp. 264, 296–298.

The Disappearance of God, a Divine Mystery

– BY –

Richard Elliott Friedman

The laws of science break down, human intellect is stymied, and one simply cannot speak of what came before the Big Bang. Cosmologists speak of the point as infinitely dense and of space as infinitely curved. Laypersons can barely comprehend what that means, and the scientists who do comprehend it still also comprehend that it means the final barrier, which beyond this point nothing can be known. The primordial point in the Kabbalistic conception likewise comes from the infinite (Ein Sof), and, as the Big Bang point is beyond inquiry through scientific channels, the Kabbalah point is beyond inquiry through religious channels. So Scholem says:

> ...*Ein Sof* cannot be subject to religious investigation, which can conceive of God only in His external aspect.

Isaiah Tishby speaks of:

> The absolute concealment of *En-Sof*....As far as *En-Sof*, the hidden God, is concerned, the mystery is

one of non-knowledge and non-perception.

And the Zohar itself says:

Beyond that point, nothing is known. So it is called Beginning.

Speaking for myself, I find the parallels in the essential elements of these two systems to be intriguing and mysterious. [Paul] Davies warns that "most scientists have a deep distrust of mysticism." And, as if to demonstrate that point, he covers mysticism (which he combines with inspiration) in three and a half pages. Distrust and skepticism are necessary and appropriate tools of honest inquiry, but one also should not exclude the possibility that there is something to be learned from this. I realize that many persons may be satisfied to dismiss the similarity of Big Bang and Kabbalah as coincidence, which it may be; but, even if we were to assume that it is strictly coincidence, we must admit that, as coincidences go, this is a multifaceted and fascinating one. At the very least, I believe it can be instructive. And at most, well, the sky's the limit.

Excerpted from *The Disappearance of God, A Divine Mystery* (Boston: Little, Brown, 1995), pp. 236–237.

We Are the Emergent Spirit of God

– BY –

John Fowler

My mother was a minister for the Unity School of Christianity, my first and most influential spiritual teacher, and the spark that ignited many subsequent years of search, contemplation and meditation. Born into a home rife with hidden alcoholism (so prevalent at the turn of the last century) and being a woman of indomitable spirit, she, in her owns words, "talked with spirit." So from an early age I was taught to do the same. I was taught to talk to my body, in sickness and in health, and to recognize the Christ Spirit, as she called it, which is within every human being. One of my earliest insights came when I was seven or eight years of age in Sunday school where we were reading about a boy stuck in the bottom of a well. Our teacher posed this question: "Could this boy pray?" My answer, both then and now, has been, "Yes because God is everywhere." Hence a new cosmology, one that proclaims a universe of omnipresent psychic and creative dimensions inherent in its very fiber, has been easy to assimilate. I suspect that such is the case for a great many people.

When I sat down to reflect on the nature of God in

light of the new cosmology it became clear that the God of which we speak is an intimate God, just as the God of an emergent universe is intimate with each of us. We are an emanation, an extension of that God in physical form. We are the emergent spirit of that God moving to realize our Divinity in sentient and well-measured form. We are that God looking for ways to express and celebrate, to show who we are, in a way that uplifts all of the earth community and even, perhaps, beyond.

Ruusbroec notes that this essential unity of our spirit "renders us neither holy nor blessed, for all person, both good and bad, possess this unity within themselves; it is, however, the first principle of all holiness and blessedness. This, then, is the meeting and union between God and our spirit in our bare nature" (*The Spiritual Espousals*, p. 118).

The Body of God:
An Ecological Theology

– BY –

Sallie McFague

God as the embodied spirit of the universe is a personal/organic model that is compatible with interpretations of both Christian faith and contemporary science, although not demanded by either. It is a way of speaking of God's relation to all matter, all creation, that "makes sense" in terms of an incarnational understanding of Christianity and an organic interpretation of postmodern science. It helps us to be whole people within our faith and within our contemporary world. Moreover, the model does not reduce God to the world nor relegate God to another world; on the contrary, it radicalizes both divine immanence (God is the breath of each and every creature) and divine transcendence (God is the energy empowering the entire universe). Finally, it underscores our bodiliness, our concrete physical existence and experience that we share with all other creatures; it is a model on the side of the well-being of the planet, for it raises the issue of ethical regard toward all bodies as all are interrelated and interdependent...

To contemplate divine transcendence as radically and concretely embodied means, of course, that it is not one thing: divine transcendence, in this model, would be in the differences, in the concrete embodiments, that constitute the universe. It is not the oneness or unity that causes us to marvel at creation, but the age, size, diversity, complexity that the common creation story tells us about. If God in the procreative-emanationist model is not primarily the initiator of creation (the simplicity of the Big Bang), but the empowering, continuing breath of life throughout its billions of years of history and in each and every entity and life-form on every star and planet, then it is in the differences that we see the glory of God. God is many, not one, for the body of God is not one body (except as a universe), but the infinite number of bodies, some living and some not, that are the universe. To know God in this model is to contemplate, reflect on the multitude of bodies in all their diversity that mediate, incarnate, the divine. Once again, there is no way to God except by way of the back. Or to put in more traditional terms, there is no way to divine transcendence except immanently...

The motifs in this passage have been central to our reflections on a model for expressing the God-world relationship in our time. This organic-agential, procreative-emanationist, body-spirit model underscores creation as the continuing, dynamic, growing embodiment of God, a body given life and power for the evolution of billions of diverse entities and creatures. This body is but the backside of God, not the face; it is the visible, mediated form of God, one that we are invited to contemplate for intimations of divine transcendence. It is a concrete, radical, immanently embodiment of God's glory, magnificence, and power. We see this transcendence immanence, this immanental transcendence, in the intricate veins of a maple leaf supplied with the water of life, in the picture from space of our blue-green marble of a planet, and in the eyes of a hungry child.

"And in the eyes of a hungry child": the model presses us not only to marvel at the wonders of the diverse, complex universe and especially our planet, but also to identify with – and suffer with – bodies in pain. If God is physical, if the universe is God's body, then the beauty and the vulnerability of bodies, the aesthetic and the ethical unite.

...For this tradition (and others as well) will suggest what certainly cannot be read off or even imagined from the story of evolution or even from the model of the world as God's body: the goal or purpose of creation is love.

Excerpted from *The Body of God; An Ecological Theology* (Minneapolis: Augsburg Fortress, 1993), pp. 150, 156–157

PART TWO
Why Are We Here?

Pilgrim   M. Honore, CSJ

Why Are We Here?

– BY –

Catherine Browning

Why are we here?
Deliver us a line.
About purpose and meaning,
And the role of humankind.
Are we here to have dominion,
Are we here to pass a test,
Are we here to celebrate the Universe,
In conscious self awareness?
Weave a tale for us,
Spin a metaphor or two,
About the grandeur of creation,
From the quantum point of view.

Our human species lives on this one planet, a pinprick in the overall scope of the universe. According to present-day scientific thought, each of us exists as the center of that universe. As that center, we each see everything as being around *us* and expanding out from *us* – and expanding out from every aspect of the universe. Everything is the center. We perceive ourselves as the center of a vast universe. From this position, looking out, and looking very small in comparison, we ask why we are here.

The wisdom gained by living on this planet for over a half-century has not answered this question for me. One answer being offered is that we are here for the survival and reproduction of our species. The belief that self-perpetuation is our purpose is like saying that the reason we have a savings account is so we have a place to deposit money. A *function* of existence is not a *purpose* for existence.

While the human mind evolved locally with its experiences limited to its sensory faculties, the technology of recent years has broadened our ability to reach beyond our tribal origins: the train and automobile, telephone and wireless communication, radio and television, airplanes and satellites, computers and web pages. While these technologies have connected us to a broader range of information and geography, it still does not tell us why we are here. We continue to struggle with the larger meaning and purpose of the human species.

When I imagine the universe, and the Earth's position within it, I am led to consider that our reason for being is limited to our place on the Earth. It is hard for me to believe that we have a significant place in the expansive universe.

In this ecosphere, we humans and the planet are one. The Earth is of substance, and we are the consciousness of that substance. This places us in a very special role within the Earth community, and it is why we are here.

Our consciousness makes us curious and creative. We are aware and wonder at our surroundings, which tantalize our senses and leave us in awe. And so the search is part of "why we are here."

To relate to the Earth and universe and explore them as deeply as we can, this is why we are here.

To connect with fellow members of our species and other species and attempt to understand them within the Earth context, this is why we are here.

To celebrate, to grieve, to experience the range of emotions that are part of us, this is why we are here.

The following articles are a response to the curiosity and creativity of persons who have chosen to explore the question of why we are here. May you enjoy their exploration, and find input into your own search for an answer.

CHAPTER THREE

Why Are We Here:
A Personal Perspective

A Fulfillment
of the Great Story

– AN INTERVIEW WITH –
Joanna Macy

What are your images of life? Why are we here?

Macy: We are here as a fruit of the great story, the unfolding of the universe. We are here to celebrate that and to evolve it further. Such celebration involves awe and great humility because it is forever beyond our complete understanding. Think of that relation of part to whole; the part can never fully understand the whole and is meant to live in harmony with it and to not cause harm. We are here to take part in the great dance of creation with the particular abilities that life has evolved in us.

How do these images affect your everyday life?

Macy: It helps me stay sane in a society that is increasingly myopic and destructive. It helps me stay sane in a society ruled by fear, greed and hatred, which is really what drives the industrial growth society. This vision helps me keep my eyes open. It gives me courage to keep on loving life and to take part in all efforts to respect it.

A Passion to Create, Celebrate, and Explore

John Fowler

Above all else God is unlimited in its creation. A dying Treya Wilber saw life as offering us the possibility of incarnating both equanimity and passion – a passion to create, celebrate and explore ourselves, vis-à-vis the wonders of our own life, and a calmness to see it through. A God co-expansive with the creation of the cosmos must be like that – serene and dettached to the outcomes of its oceanic creative consciousness which birthed a cosmic sea full of ripples and droplets, each of them rubbing, hugging, and shifting into one another. That same ocean would mount its own tide regardless of those who are swept to her shores by the same patterns and motions that ensured her own life-giving survival and the survival of those who have graciously and tenaciously adapted to her storms, flow, and rhythm.

Within this frothy sea of consciousness and realization we find surprise, jostling, and compassion for all the drops of water that have become the ocean and that live within us. All of them will become part of the great cycle of water, rising as clouds, falling as rain, and then running to the sea as the eager lifeblood of our planet.

They will change their form, their temperature, environment, but not their cycle of life-giving movement. In that, they are similar to the bacteria. Will the bacterial consciousness of our bodies ever perish? As a local event, certainly, but what of the consciousness of all bacteria, inseparable from the planet and maybe even life itself? And what, the skeptic may ask, of the possibility of extinction? Will that consciousness, or more correctly those acts of bacterial cognition that avoid harm, move toward survival and sharing without limit just as our star has shared more than four billion years of her life with us? We know not what these bacteria are, so constant is their exchange of information, memory, and hence experience, but I believe that these tiny friends are but a tiny trillionth of a trillionth of the manifestations of a divine universe forever seeking to express itself. They have a kind of intentionality, a behavior that is directed toward an end and toward the objects of those ends. In their case that intention may well be unrealized. As we continually move toward greater and greater mental and spiritual encounters we become ever more aware that our intentions are becoming more clear. But then, I must ask, "Are our intentions ever truly separate from those of the universe in which we live? Are we, like the sun and the bacteria, part of a greater whole? Are we not capable of at least a preliminary map of this brave and exciting New World?"

Credo

– BY –
Evelyn Pease Tyner

We are born human beings
in a vast, unfolding,
omnicentric universe,
members of Earth's community,
kin to a myriad of beings
diverse, unique,
living and dying,
evolving.
Trembling with consciousness
we explore
realms of beauty,
complexity, history,
forgiven-ness,
and joy.
We acknowledge
that within our species
evil is real
and violence rampant.

That, however, does not excuse us
from the effort to transform
tribal viciousness and cruelty
to compassion.
Our task is to be aware,
learn,
seek justice and peace,
work creatively,
celebrate,
wonder,
and love.

Continuing the Loving Creation

– AN INTERVIEW WITH –

Brooke Medicine Eagle

Why are we here?

Medicine Eagle: We are here to continue the loving creation that Creator began. We're an extension of that process into the material world. All of us, every being, everything is. We two-legged beings, we humans, seem to have been given an extra level of possibility in creating things, an absolutely infinite variety of creative possibilities. The human experience is an experiment on freedom; we've been given the freedom to act in any way we choose. I believe we're here to show love really does work and to express that into the world. We are here to remember ourselves as One with creation, to live open-hearted, heart-centered, loving, trusting and cooperating with the world. This will allow an exquisite blossoming of all life on Earth.

Dawn Star, the Christ figure in the Americas, taught us what our native people call *Flower Song*. That *Flower Song* is about a flowering of the Earth and of each individual. I believe that the blossoming comes when we love and support each other, and help everyone feel secure and free. When they feel this way, humans have an easy time expressing more and more of the beauty they are. We must call forward the finest and best from everyone's heart. Eventually we will all get clear that coming back into the wholeness, the holiness of which White Buffalo Calf Woman speaks, is the goal.

Creator guarantees that even as we move back into that wholeness and Oneness, we don't lose our individually creative selves. There is a paradoxical, but incredibly positive blending of the Oneness and individual expression, that we are guaranteed through this covenant. Something far beyond our logical mind, which is eternal life, where we are totally present in the now and yet go on and on and on in a creative manner that is more amazing than we can believe. Although we may be here on this Earth plane, there are universes and possibilities untold and unlimited.

We must lift ourselves up and find the joy of acting in love, wholeness and holiness. I tell my students that the Great Spirit is the Great Spirit, not the Great Serious. Life is about joy, and aliveness and richness and play and celebration and spirit; that is the spiritual process.

Why Are We Here?

– BY –

Marlaina Kreinin

Why and why and why
Are we here on this Earth?
It is to give birth
To a never-ending dream
Of the possible,
Of what we can become.

It is to give voice
To the beauty of choice,
The challenge and glory
Of what being human
Can truly be,
Realized in its total splendor,

The finest specimen of humankind
Is one who loves and lives with grace,
Striving to partner with the Divine
Making the Earth
A place of paradise
Which in truth we were given.

"Correct, Sit Down, Next"

– BY –

Peggy Logue

Why are we here? As a child I learned a very clear answer to this question. I learned the first day I entered Catholic schools. It was our daily religion drill and you had better be prepared. The nuns would ask you to stand to recite your answer and no one was excused. You felt shame if you did not know the answer. Then you were quickly dismissed as the next child recited her answer. It was done in rows, seat by seat. Students attending Catholic schools will remember the *Baltimore Catechism* drills. The question then was, "Why did God make you?" The answer, "God made me to know, love, and serve Him in this world, and to be happy with Him in the next." Mother Church would be sure we knew how to do this. Catholics will also remember the familiar follow up... "Correct, sit down, next."

I don't know that the answer is much different today. But because of our evolved knowledge and awareness of the expanding universe the meaning of the words have expanded to a deeper level. I don't know that I personally and truly know why we are here or why anything is here. Experiences in my life's journey peel back layer by layer from this mystery, revealing more and more to me.

But to think I have a real handle on the deepest meaning of why we are here would not be honest. From my head knowledge and what I have felt in my heart some things seem to be real. I am here "knowing." Thomas Berry says, "By bringing forth the planet Earth, its living forms, and its human intelligence, the universe has found, so far as we know, its most elaborate expression and manifestation of its deepest mystery. Here, in its human mode, the universe reflects on and celebrates itself in a unique mode of conscious self-awareness." This statement challenges my thinking. To begin to grasp it I must see myself as part of and not separate from the universe or any of creation. It assumes an intimacy with the universe. I am one with, and I am the reflecting self-conscious awareness of, the universe. The human being is that dimension of the universe that is reflecting on itself. We are the universe! We are thinking about, feeling, tasting, seeing and touching and reflecting on ourselves. The Creative Force initialing the flaring forth, birthing the universe, also birthed the human with intelligence and conscious awareness. This conscious awareness is our human "knowing that we know" and reflective self-awareness. We are the universe "knowing." We know that we were brought forth as the most "elaborate expression and manifestation of its deepest mystery." As the universe reflecting on itself, we have come to the awareness that all of creation came from One. We are here knowing deeply and knowing intimately the sacredness of all of creation. We are here "knowing" and telling the sacred story. We are here telling the story of "knowing."

Love can be expressed with words such as *intimacy*, *allurement*, and *communion*. Love awakens in the knowing.

We do not love what we do not know. There is a saying that we fear what we do not know, and what we fear we hate, and what we hate we destroy. Is it because we have separated ourselves from Earth and have forgotten the story that we are destroying so much of Earth? We began intimately with her and all of creation having the same ancient history in stardust. Sacredness is apparent as we remember this. Earth allures me with beautiful sunsets, cathedral pine groves and light-sparkled streams, eagles in flight and wolves and bears in wilderness, and I am called to tears with reverence. I connect with these experiences as a participant as well as a conscious reflective being. I am allured and alluring. Yet there is a pain inside me that only tears can express as I consider Earth and the devastation upon her. It is painful to be part of the devastation. It is also humbling because I know I am part of it. While I am part of the devastation I am also being devastated. I know of the integration and communion of all life as the community of one. I know that what happens to one part happens to all. I believe that all creation is a expression of "One" and love has no place for me to separate myself from this "One." Therefore, I hold all in reverence and respect and do nothing that would bring separation, harm or destruction. In my knowing Earth, my most intimate experience of the universe, I succumb to her allurement and relate intimately in communion. In this "knowing" and "loving" my deepest needs are met. I am here, loving and being loved, although I may fall short, my awareness continues to deepen. I am the universe knowing and loving. I have a particular role to fulfill as the evolving knowing and loving universe. I have a certain work. Whatever it is I must bring it to light just as the tree exults in being a tree, I must celebrate my humanness in being what I am called to be. This is what I am and what I do will enrich the life of all other beings here and into the future. We are here to love and to tell the story of loving.

We can be awestruck by the great mystery of life as it is revealed in nature. The changing seasons, the miracle of birth, the power of waves crashing on the shore, the call of majestic mountains, the love we feel for others, the cycle of birth and death and rebirth. We are carried to depths of uncertainty in the pain of life as it is reflected in our suffering. We suffer loss of loved ones, our health our financial security, our earth home.

Our spirits soar with creativity as we begin to heal from our wounds and open up new opportunities in our life to our greatness. What we have learned in life is transformed into serving all of creation. Our knowing, which comes from the experience of awe and the pain in our life, is reformed through love reflected in our creative response and celebrated in communion with the created universe. Serving is being compassionate. Compassion is the highest form of love. It is the goal of all religious traditions. We are here serving, being compassion. We are here celebrating compassion in a universe of community. Compassion is passionately being our knowing, loving and serving for the benefit of all creation now and in the future. We are here serving and telling the story of compassion.

We are the universe " knowing" itself as the manifestation of the Creative Force that brought all into being. We are the universe "loving," having an intimate relationship with all of creation choosing only that which is for the enhancement of all of creation. We are the universe "serving" by being compassion... that is celebrating creation in its fullness and beauty as one community in love with itself.

Why are we here? We are the universe knowing, loving and serving itself here in this time, so that we and all of the created, now and in future generations, may hear the story, know the story, love the story, share the story and be the story.

"Correct, sit down, next!"

Why We Humans Are on Earth
– I Know the Answer

– BY –

David Haenke

I know the answer to the question of why we human beings are on the Earth. But I can't say I answered it first. Thomas Berry answered it first. Before the punchline let me give a little eco-theological exegesis...

Thomas Berry may or may not be eventually recognized by any significant percentage of human beings in his rightful place as among the handful of the greatest minds that ever minded on this Earth, but his life and work are a personification of our purpose here on the garden planet. Before he became the first Eco-logian, he was probably the world's foremost interpreter of his fellow Catholic cleric, Teilhard de Chardin. In the preface to Chardin's astounding *Phenomenon of Man*, one of the Huxleys (I forget which) defined the human in the context of the book: Humankind is evolution become conscious of itself. So here it is: Chardin tells us *what we are*. (As "evolution" is no more or less than the story of the Earth/ecology.) We are a certain kind of reflective consciousness, one now aware of our evolution (within Evolution), but, it turns out, astounding as it is, we must not (as we rampantly do) over-value and become arrogantly obsessed about this unique attribute, especially since it has yet to attain sanity – the elemental sanity of its Earthly origin.

Chardin first told the universe story – intending a religio-scientific context – of the human "cosmogenesis," but he told it, despite his "Christianity," in purely anthropocentric terms, and his "omega point," the end point of evolution, the self-realization of the noosphere into collective consciousness, was really an apotheosis of the human. (Berry wrote a brilliant essay on the New Age movement in the early 80s, where he identified Chardin as its principle source, and referred to it as the "cult of the ultra-human".)

Berry's body of work as born-again Eco-Logian took him far beyond the anthropocentrism of Chardin. Indeed, Thomas has made a profound "course correction" on Chardin. Thomas recognized that, whether we know it or like it or not, we are in what he calls "the ecozoic age," where, if we are to survive, we have to realize, and act constructively upon the realization that ecological reality is in immediate, imminent and complete control of our individual and collective existence, holding all the keys to our continued evolution and existence on the planet.

As I would interpret Thomas Berry through my own Earthly work: The purpose of our existence is to love, honor, celebrate, constantly and prayerfully give thanks and appreciation for, actively and reverentially care for, and recognize as our ultimate teacher, and healer – the Earth, in this ecozoic age. Further, to fully realize this, we must "re-invent" (Thomas's word) ourselves as a species, shift from our present terminal, autistic anthropocentrism to a full-on eco-centrism. This shift is so profound, so epochal, that it in itself constitutes the "re-invention".

I call the re-invention the genesis of "eco-sapiens." Anthropocentrism – a "hall of mirrors" – is the heart of the deep, deadly, suicidal madness of the human species in its negative mutation into the exterminating bio-mechanism I call "homo-techo-industrialis," and what I believe Thomas is referring to in discussing the present "civilization" as collectively "autistic." Anthropocentrism is individual/collective ecological autism. The shift out of anthropocentrism constitutes a favorable mutation into virtually a new species: eco-sapiens in the Ecozoic Age and the first genesis of species sanity. The degree of sanity and intelligence is ultimately defined by the degree of ecological awareness and practice. The depth of the stupidity and insanity of present day "civilized life" is here illumined.

My work on Earth is essentially to initiate the implementation, in physical reality, of Thomas's vision. I am here to do all I can to implement the meaning of why I am here. This, in a nutshell, means the relentless advocacy of using the Earth's greenprints: the application of the flawless, billions-years old, sun-driven, miraculously efficient, godlike ecological design principles and practices at every level and aspect of human life – technology, economics, politics, religion, transportation, agriculture, all of it, every bit of it. A little slogan that I use: "To do all things ecologically, everywhere." That work proceeds in about thirty dimensions.

Eco-theologically, the total (timeless span of infinite numbers of miracles constituting one vast ongoing Miracle) reality of the Earth abundantly fulfills all human descriptions of "God," and we come from and are a part of this great being, body, soul, and spirit. For those human faith traditions that are unable to ascribe holiness to the Earth I say this: "If you can't say that the Earth is holy, then you must live your life as though it is." Back to relentlessly anthropocentric faith traditions, all say the Earth/Creation is a creation of God, and within this there is no way to get around that this Earth Creation is an extension of God, as in the Christian Bible where it is said, "The Earth is the Lord's and the fruits thereof." Thou shalt not despoil the Earth. The Earth comes from God and doesn't belong to us and it's a sin to despoil it. Like sanity and intelligence, God, good, sin and evil are really defined ecologically, where (infinitely beyond a mere "science") ecology represents the full reality of the Earth.

The expression of divinity of the "god-like" in human beings comes only from acting out of fusion with our own ecological reality as we are an extension and organelle of that of the Earth, in living practice of our purpose here as described before. (Conscious anti-ecological action constitutes a definition of alien evil, and unconscious anti-ecological action – innocent or not – does its work, thanklessness and insatiability a strong part of this entropic all.)

Humans on Earth

– BY –

Meg Hanrahan

Humans are on earth to participate in the spiral dance of creation. This belief, shared by many Earth-centered cultures, sees creation as an ongoing, ever-unfolding event, is nurtured along and supported by human inter-action in the process. Life must be renewed, and humans must work to renew it. In this dance of creation, we sup-port the Earth, and the Earth supports us in a mutual reciprocal dynamic relationship.

How do we participate then? How might we fulfill our purpose with actions and activities that nurture life and creation? I believe we do this by first placing our-selves in the proper context, by remembering ourselves as a part of nature, as a species of Earth. From this "grounded" place, we might realize our meaning and purpose, our connection to past and future generations of humans, our connection to other Earth species. We might find happiness, health, and well-being. We might move beyond our present discontent and alienation to find ourselves at home in the world we live in.

Specifically, we can do this by engaging consciously in the rhythms and processes of the natural world:

- By celebrating the seasons, becoming aware of the solstices, equinoxes, and cross-quarter days and their significance and meaning: by engaging in seasonal activities with awareness and reverence. For instance, by planting seeds in the spring we can become the goddess, enacting the creation story in a very real way. Each season has its special lessons, gifts, mysteries – it is our task to witness, to engage, to celebrate these.
- By following the cycles of the moon, becoming sensitive to the moon rhythms in our bodies, feeling the ebb and flow of the tides in our lives each month.
- By embracing the elements of nature as our gods and our guides, and other Earth species as our brothers and our sisters. We have so much to learn from these other earth entities, so much to be grateful for in their presence.
- By preserving and protecting the earth and our natural resources.
- By growing gardens and caring for natural spaces.
- By learning from our ancestors, and by teaching our children how to walk the Earth with honor and respect. Doing this, we might in essence create a continuum of humans connected to the universal energy, caring for the Earth.
- By giving ourselves opportunities to feel awe and wonder as we look upon any of the many faces of the goddess in nature.
- By celebrating the beauty and mystery of life – with song, dance, art and ritual, for instance.
- By creating communities that share Earth-centered values.
- By using our imaginations to create solutions that help to heal the earth.

These are some of the many ways we might reengage in the ever-evolving process of creation. We are key players in the drama. But our contribution has been lacking; we have forgotten our part. By immersing ourselves in reverence and respect, awe and wonder, commitment and caring, in the sensorial magic of the living universe, we might find our place and our purpose in life renewed. Then we might hope to fulfill our part in the renewal of creation.

The Kinglet at the Door

– BY –

K. Lauren De Boer

Once for each thing. Just once; no more. And we too, just once. And never again.
—Rainer Maria Rilke, "Ninth Elegy"

This ramshackle writer's cabin works well for me. It is nestled in the hillside above the flat that empties into Tomales Bay. The area, mostly ranchland, is being returned to wetlands, I'm told. A few dairy cows are sequestered on the far side of the valley, an odd picture of domesticity against the backdrop of wild and primal Point Reyes National Seashore. The weather has been wonderfully erratic—alternating wind and rain with sun and fog, all amidst dramatic shifts of light.

There are candles mounted on the braces and struts of the cabin, heavy tools on the walls—bal pein hammers, an axe, a pipe wrench, hedge clippers. These hand tools remind me that I am here to work with the tools of the word. Their presence makes me feel the heftiness that the craft of language carries. I feel the urge to grasp and wield, tuning the fine bolt of a phrase, trimming an awkward sentence.

There is a space heater at my feet, two lamps, two pine desks, two doors opening to the south and to the west, and a balcony I can walk out onto to stretch and feel the wind. A wooden chair on the deck invites me to go out—so I can go in.

Birds swarm around the cabin like gnats to a cow. Last night, just at dusk, a Cooper's hawk perched on the railing of the balcony not five feet from me. I had ample time to take in his wild feathered beauty. Then he dropped and glided into the bramble, where moments before I had seen a salon of hermit thrushes.

White egrets power their way over the plain like pure thoughts, angelic and untouchable. Watching their flight distills my thinking. They light on the wetlands and the land and waters come to exquisite attention. Vultures circle over the vast green, searching for the fallen, leaving signs that the living don't want to admit to consciousness. The crows, in their iridescent black, seem the antithesis of the egrets—playful, demonic, steeped in the imperfect, tumbling in delight with Earth's constant creative surges.

I prefer the crows. They somehow occupy, live, the space between immanent and transcendent, independent and raucous in their irreverence. Their intelligence exhilarates me. I want to be part of their clan. They seem to know what's suspect and what to accept all in the same moment. They are solitary, or they flock in the hundreds, depending on what suits them. Crows talk to each other constantly, have elaborate communication systems, even on the wing. They don't worry for tomorrow. They tumble with the wind like black scarves abandoned to chance.

I stand to stretch, open the cabin door, and find a ruby-crowned kinglet dead on the doormat. Is this why the vultures have been venturing so near the cabin? I bend down to pick him up, and as I touch the kinglet, I feel irreverent. My movements seem too clumsy and too swift to impart the tenderness I feel. I can't help it—I feel the same paternal tenderness toward all animals, birds especially.

There isn't a mark on his amazingly tiny body. His head is cocked back, leading me to believe that he broke his neck flying into the window. I marvel at his lightness and at the coldness of his body, so soon after death. Most beings are heavy at death, as if they were yearning to be drawn back into the Earth.

The subtle flicker of a ruby streak on the crown of the kinglet's head flares up to a blaze underneath when I part the feathers. Kinglets are nicely named, both for their color and for the royal designation. I have always been drawn to them for this reason. Kinglet: a small king. Like rivulet, a small river. They are tiny birds—our smallest next to hummingbirds and bushtits—yet stunning and ferocious in their drab beauty. A white eye ring intensifies their gaze into a disarming curiosity.

Kinglet song is imposing for the size of its creator. One field guide describes the kinglet's song as "wheezy and subdued." This does an inept disservice to a Herculean singer. The song is a remarkable outburst, loud and rich, peaking with a rollicking tee-da-leet, tee-da-leet, tee-da-leet. Kinglets revel in throwing their song to the world. In revealing themselves, questions of size or self-doubt are not in their repertoire.

Ruby-crowned kinglets are lucky to live four years.

Vultures pass shadows over the cabin endlessly. One

cruises my window with a dead rodent in its beak, taunting me to distraction. Yesterday my writing wheeled around death as if to mimic the vultures. Today, I find death deposited neatly at my door in the form of a kinglet. I seem destined to face mortality on this retreat. It's as if the Earth is telling me to pay attention. Time to stop writing in circles and deliver up a package.

If I truly believed in my own death, I wouldn't waste time with doubt, I would just write. As Rilke writes in the *Ninth Elegy*, "Once for each thing. Just once; no more. And we too, just once. And never again." My rough translation: "Now is my time to be Lauren."

The vultures are thickening in numbers and intensity outside the cabin. Something draws them beyond the willow thicket outside my window. They encroach and press in, the sound of their wings the music of my own dying. I try to let the fluttering leaves of the alders drown out the dour birds. But when they do, I hear the same song, even as the leaves shudder with joy. Joy sings out of the breast of death. It is the sound I am drawn to for my survival, for the marrow of my living.

"Here is the time for the sayable," wrote Rilke, "here is its homeland. Speak and bear witness."

If Ruby, as I have now come to call the kinglet on the desk in front of me, had not appeared, had not come to me in death, I may not have spoken: "Kinglet, Ruby-crowned. Too-short life abandoned."

> *How can my heart praise invisibly*
> *The world as it arises within me*
> *How can I hear the green Earth*
> *And see the caw of the crow*

And so satisfy the call of the seraphim—
Holy! Holy! Holy!

There must be some other sense
I can pierce the world with,
Shedding my blindness
To what is so near at hand
A revelation, born of a new organ
With which to know mystery.

Each time I look at Ruby, I feel gratitude. Something wells in me that makes me feel more at home. The way Ruby was laid at my doorstep was like a gift left for a starving prisoner. In a sense I am starving. And I am a prisoner. I hunger, as we all do, for home and place. I feel the pangs of longing for beauty, to never shut down my inner gateway to wonder, at being stunned or terrified. Ruby, here beside my writing pad, makes me feel truly liberated as only the sense of the presence of death, can.

Hunger and imprisonment are not essential to who I am. They are states of mind I induce when I forget and fear. Gratitude dissolves our forgetfulness and returns us home to Earth and each other. There are ruby-crowned kinglets. And alders, vultures, egrets. Just once, and no more.

My kind is now the perpetrator of a great vanishing from the Earth. There is no time to waste. The story strains to be heard. My kind also has a unique evolutionary heritage: to speak and bear witness. And for this, I can feel fortunate to be in the world. For this, I am human.

A Feeling for the Whole

– BY –

Gwen Gordon

Sitting out on the grass on a moonless, cloudless night I gaze at the arch of the Milky Way, letting the forms of beloved constellations reveal themselves in the wealth of the luminaries. I sink back into a happy sense of my own nothingness before the certainty of the stars. I do not experience terror at this vastness of space-time but an aspect of immensity that is comforting – all those stars and all the invisible worlds beyond them are necessary for me to have come into existence. I *am* this immensity gazing into itself, born from the fire of its stars and cooled down enough to be able to think, see and admire. No matter how remote these distant ancestors are, in this moment I know that we would not *be* without each other and that we are now becoming only by means of each other. A sense of awe sweeps through me.

Still shimmering with the warmth of communion I go to my car, turn the ignition key and put my foot on the gas. Instantly, I feel a sharp stab in my heart. I take my foot off the gas and the pain goes away. I'm not thinking about CO_2 emissions and the greenhouse effect, nor how there are too many cars and how driving alienates us from nature. I am not in this moment an environmentalist, a social critic, or a cosmologist. I am life pained by an act of violence against itself. From the sensitivity I feel, giving up driving is not a sacrifice for the greater good, it is simply an act of love.

Love has everything to do with the perpetuation of life. The sensitivities that love awakens and the love that sensitivities awaken are the vehicles by which we carry on the evolutionary journey and become fully human. Most of our species have evolved the capacity to sense and as a result, understand and love only our most immediate physical and emotional world. However, it is only by awakening our sensitivities to the whole of life, past, present, and future, that we have a chance of finding our way through the dire epistemological and ecological crises we face.

From our current depth and scope of sensitivity our attempts to fix things only make them worse. We are such an intricately interconnected network of patterns on the scale of the global ecology, that neither reasoning faculties nor feeling faculties alone are adequate for the job. We need our existing capacities to be vitalized, deepened, and tuned to the depths of the universe and new subtle capacities to be awakened.

We do not have to have a big master plan. But we do have to listen to the knot in our hearts, the roar in our throats, the goose bumps on our arms, and inquire deeply into them to find the guidance we need moment to moment. This is the genius of the whole universe, as close to us as our own body/minds. And if we are to sustain the life of the planet, fulfill our evolutionary destiny and liberate our deepest creativity, it is our singular task to awaken these sensitivities – on behalf of all that has been, all that is, and all that might become through us.

All beings are unique fields of sensitivities. Sensitivities are what make a flatworm different from Picasso, a heron different from Bill Gates. They are the fruit of evolution and the earmark of individuality. The more complex the life, the more developed and finely tuned its sensitivities. Our sensitivities are the living, sizzling universe within us as well as our means of embracing, articulating, enhancing, elaborating and adoring that universe. What distinguishes humans from a slime mold is not only the range, power, and expression of our sensitivities but our ability to self-sensitize, to consciously increase or diminish our sensitivity to the Whole. This is one of the most direct and powerful ways we can participate in the evolution of the cosmos.

Sensing the Whole does not require nightly meditations on the Milky Way. What it does require is the development, liberation, and exquisite tuning of all our perceptions toward dimensions that are not available through ordinary experience.

Learning to sense the Whole:

- Requires that we become devoted students of life's patterns, rhythms and forms.
- It requires inhabiting our full fifteen-billion-year-old, evolving story so that the resources of our deep memory – its myths, songs, stories, and dreams – are available to our imaginations.
- It requires inhabiting deep time so that both our far distant ancestors and the yet-to-be-born are real to us.
- It requires fully inhabiting our animal bodies to resonate and feel with the core of all life.

- And it requires the liberation of the artful, sponta-
neous creative play within us, through which love
finds its myriad forms.
- It is to dwell in the silence through which we are
able to create ourselves and our world moment to
moment without getting attached to our plans, our
desires, and our perspectives.
- And it is recognizing moment to moment the identity we share with the whole of creation – such that
our thoughts sympathetically resonate with the deep
structures of the world, our bodies move in its
rhythms, and all our actions celebrate and enhance
its life and beauty.

The word *whole* is misleading, for we imagine a big,
finished, undivided thing just waiting to be compre-
hended. But there is no "whole" that isn't itself continuously evolving through our perception of it. We participate deeply in the universe by evoking its subtlety and
complexity through our very sensitivity to it.

We Are Expressions of God

– AN INTERVIEW WITH –

Virginia Froehle

Why are we here?

Froehle: As the life of the Sacred Mystery flows into us, we become expressions, words, of God. Our purpose is to express those qualities, aspects, faces of the Sacred which flow into us and through us to others. We can block the Divine in ourselves. It is blocked in some ways in just about everyone at sometime, usually in childhood. (I think that might be what we name "original sin.") We are called to move through the blocks and open ourselves to be fuller expressions of the Divine Love and Goodness.

What you say is somewhat abstract. How do you decide how to live your life?

Froehle: I believe that the will of God is the good of ourselves, of others and the world in which we live. So I orient my living that way. When I fail, I refocus.

I have an enthusiastic interest in all kinds of religions and, the more I read, the more I find that the teachings and ways of Jesus make the most sense to me. He is my model in knowing and living what is good. He is my model in my suffering. Jesus never told us why suffering exists, but he showed us how to deal with it. Rather than walk away from it, try to rise above it, ignore it, cover it up with drugs or distracting behaviors, he walked into it with faith in his caring parent, Abba. In doing so, he came out of the suffering into new life.

CHAPTER FOUR
Why Are We Here:
A Universal Perspective

Who Are We?

– BY –

Diarmuid O'Murchu

Nearly all the great religions offer a similar answer to
that question: "To praise, honour, and glorify God." The
problem with that answer is its patriarchal undertones.
God is perceived, indeed projected, as a mighty Lord and
Ruler, omniscient, omnipotent, one to whom we owe
unquestioned loyalty. All these characteristics say a great
deal more about power-hungry humans than about the
nature of the divine. They are not so much features of
revealed truth as projections of the compulsive need to
dominate and control. Very rightly, modern writers such
as Easterbrook[1] and Chopra[2] alert us to the human projections on which we have construed this idolatrous divine edifice. Sadly, all the major religions, to one degree
or another, are contaminated with this idolatry.

So, why are we here? The question begs a more fundamental one: "Who are we?" Quantum physics reminds
us that each one of us is a constellation of creative energy
forever fluctuating between wave and particle manifestation. Perhaps this insight gets into the mystery of our
being in a much more profound way than modern religion is capable of doing. Yes, we are energy, co-creative

energy, begotten from depths of creation in the original flaring forth of the Big Bang, but also long before it, in the fertile emptiness of divine being and becoming.

We are ageless creatures, perhaps without beginning or end! We belong to the great divine rhythm of energy that constitutes everything in creation. Many thousands of years ago, we attained an intuitive insight that this energy was a form of spirit power. Long before religion ever evolved we called this sacred energy Holy Spirit. It is the first and oldest name we humans gave to the divine life force.

And then we had another brain wave, more accurately, a heart wave! This Spirit energy seems to be forever giving birth: to stars, mountains, lakes, seasons, fireflies and daffodils! We began to envisage the life-force as a motherlike figure of prodigious creativity. Today, we refer to her as the Great Goddess that our Paleolithic ancestors worshipped for at least thirty thousand years.[3]

So, why are we here? The answer seems fairly obvious: to give birth to the divine in our world, to continue the great work of birthing-forth that our God has been about from time immemorial. Meister Eckart stated it with clarity and conviction: "What does God do all day long? God lies on a maternity bed giving birth all day long."

As a Christian people our call to birthing the new creation was described by Jesus as "the New Reign of God." It is not a reign of power, domination and glory-seeking, but one of empowering, liberating and healing for all who feel trapped in the alienation of patriarchal domination. The great tragedy, of course, is that it has taken Christianity almost two thousand years to catch up with the vision of Jesus. The Christian churches have done a very effective job in undermining the birthing power of Jesus.

In our day, this call to birthing the new creation is about justice-making more than anything else. Our suffering Earth cries out for justice; the poor of our world yearn and weep for it; the tortured animals and birds groan for it; every creature feeling oppressed hungers for it; the corruption and sleaze so rampant in modern politics and economics is living proof that such justice is long overdue.

Our anthropocentric modes of relating, even within the religions, are manipulative, crude and oppressive. Setting relationships right is the primary task of Spirit-imbued people in our age. But the relationships are not just about people; they are about every organism of creation the cosmos and home-planet included. We cannot hope to heal the fragmentation of the human spirit – until the battered, tortured Earth also knows healing.

This is a formidable task for which we have few precedents in the contemporary world. But we are creatures of an ancient, sacred story, and our religious traditions embryonically carry useful guidelines. We must not waste time trying to get it perfect; in fact this compulsive preoccupation with perfection may itself be the idolatry of this age that is crucifying our vision and paralyzing our imaginations.

---

[1]. Easterbrook, Gregg. *Beside Still Waters* (New York: William Morrow, 1998).

[2]. Chopra, Deepak. *How to Know God* (New York: Harmony Books, 2000).

[3]. More on this topic in Carol P. Christ, *Rebirth of the Goddess* (New York: Routledge, 1997).

There Is No Assigned Role

- BY -

John Seed

I don't think we have any role that has been assigned us from anywhere else. Our choice may be similar to the role of the first photosynthesizers which inadvertently created all of this oxygen thereby causing the first mass extinction and giving rise to the aerobic epoch. We may be giving rise to the radioactive epoch or some other miraculous thing, that after five or ten million years, will fully populate itself and every niche will be full. I feel that our role is innocent. I don't hold the view that we are some terrible scourge or cancer, although to ourselves and to our own future we may be. It has never been clear to me whether those early anaerobic photosynthesizers, who generated all of this oxygen, survived themselves the process. Some things obviously survived because here we are talking about them.

Robinson Jeffers says that as we speed up, we start to radiate and shine.[1]

"You making haste, haste on decay: not blameworthy." "...Meteors are not needed less than mountains: shine, perishing republic."*

So as we speed up and glow like a meteor there are no moral questions except within our own frame of reference. In the larger frame of reference creation and destruction are equal, there is not a moral side of creation. If the anaerobic bacteria had been wiped out by photosynthesis we wouldn't be here. History is written by the victors and who knows who the victors will be. Cockroaches may look back and say, "It was kind of sad for them but it was really good for us."

To the universe, humans are not needed more than ants; I feel one of the mistakes we are making is to think we are the reason all of this took place, that we are the point of the story, the stars of the show. We are not. We are swirling around like everything else. We may be in a position to forestall the closing of the Cenozoic period and preserve the Cenozoic remnant including ourselves for another fifty or one hundred million years before we become extinct and before the ants or whoever comes next take over. I'll vote for that personally. I feel like our story has just begun. The dinosaur had one hundred fifty million years. Why should we give up now because we want another hair dryer or whatever the story is? If we only understood who we are from a bigger perspective than we might be in the position to change our destiny and so change our role.

The idea found in Thomas Berry's writings is that our purpose here is to celebrate. That is a profound understanding as long as it doesn't lead to a sense of denial that here we are – mammals that have just created the conditions for the end of mammals. There is something profoundly regrettable about that. I feel that any celebration we do has to be tempered with a strong commitment to our incarnation. It is not enough to escape to that largest view and to tower beyond tragedy. We have to take strength from that largest view and dive as deep as we dare into that tragedy to attempt to avert it or at least to warn our people. I feel a little bit cautious about endorsing the kind of joy that comes from the big picture because I think it is too easy for us to hide there. That is definitely an option but I don't think that's our role.

For us to produce less of ourselves would require that a whole new level emerge. That may be what we are witnessing, the birth of this new level. It's not only the reproduction but also the accumulation. We are trying to surround ourselves with this kind of security that is an honorable acquired trait. There were those at the time of our ancestors who did not have this in a strong degree. Their babies did not have babies and so they are not around to inform the gene pool. We are descended from those creatures that did whatever they had to do to have lots of babies, following the fundamental commandment to survive, the urge to be. Now our minds tell us in order for that urge to exist, to fulfill itself, we have to do exactly the opposite of what we have done for over a million years. To make that connection between our understanding and that most primal and fundamental of all urges is even deeper than the urge to reproduce, because the urge to exist existed before there was any sex. It is not a precedent situation and I haven't received any insights or information that we are going to make it.

There is nothing else to do unless you decide to oppose that urge to exist. I believe our best chance is to want that as much as possible. But, of course, that opens us to the sorrow and pain to a deeper extent. Thich Nhat Hahn says the most important thing we can do is hear within ourselves the sounds of the Earth crying. If we are prepared to realize that we are not going to be destroyed or crushed by the suffering of our world, and if we are prepared to experience that suffering, then we are not afraid to go to that place of really wanting us to continue. It's like being in love with someone who is going to be hanged in the morning and choosing to love him/her all the more rather then to pull back.

I don't think guilt is helpful to our survival. I also don't think lashing ourselves, or despising human beings, or comparing human beings to cancer, or to bacteria on a petri dish, eating itself out of existence, or other such images are useful. I think we need to bask in the glory because it might give us a picture of how good it might feel if we can make it out of this next siege.

We are sometimes accused of not liking human beings. We did a calculation on how many human beings would fit on the planet over the next two hundred years before we wipe ourselves out. Then suppose for the sake of argument that the optimum number of human beings living sustainably on the Earth at one time is, say, 100 million and that this number of human beings will continue to thrive here for another billion or two years before the sun heats up sufficiently to make mammalian life unlikely on the Earth. In this scenario, we would get orders of magnitude more humans on the Earth. So, it is really the "business as usual" crowd who are misanthropic and we who are the true "humanists." We love humans, we'd just rather have them spread out over hundreds of millions or billions of years rather than squeeze as many as possible on the Earth for a few generations followed by none at all.

---

[1]Robinson Jeffers. "Shine Perishing Republic," *Roan Stallion, Tamar and Other Poems* (New York: Boni and Liveright, 1924).

For Wonder, Joy, Beauty, and Intimacy

– AN INTERVIEW WITH –

Thomas Berry

Why are we here?

Berry: We are here for three purposes: for joyful wonder, beauty and intimacy. We can be conscious of these in a way that other beings cannot because of their lack of what is called "reflective consciousness." That is, consciousness knowing itself as well as knowing other things. To be able to reflect on oneself is the wonder of being human. To have that capacity is what enables us to build the type of world that we build as humans through our capacity to develop sciences. We have to not only come together as a community but to organize our community, to reflect on being together and participating in our political process, social process, religious process, and to be able to shape those activities consciously. Other animals are spontaneously grouped together in herds, which form certain social patterns. But we humans select our social groups, select our forms of government, select our forms of education and in this manner we take control of our lives more than other beings can.

Now why do humans exist? Everything exists for participation and beatitude. You might say that the Divine is the quintessence of light, of beauty, of intimacy, and of wonder. These things escape our minds. We have no good way of dealing with these questions. In other words, all these questions of God, how do we think of God, how do we pray, how do we shape our lives, all these questions end with a kind of a mythic answer rather than a technical answer. There is no way of describing the communion experience even with humans in our presence to each other. We are awkward in trying to describe that relation. What's the point? I have a little verse where I answer some of these basic questions, and it goes like this,

> Look up at the sky, the heavens so blue,
> the sun so radiant, the clouds so playful,
> the soaring raptors, the meadows in bloom,
> the woodland creatures,
> the rivers singing their way to the sea,
> wolves' song on the land, whales' song on the sea,
> celebration everywhere, wild, riotous, immanence.
> A monsoon which brings an ocean of joy
> comes spilling down over the Appalachian landscape,
> drenching us all with the deluge of light
> as we open our arms and rush toward each other,
> you and I and all of us who by that vast compassionate person
> who brings all things together in intimate celebration.
> Celebration that's the universe itself.

The universe is the celebratory experience of the Divine and of creatures and that's why traditional civilizations were always created and governed by the universe as the great liturgy. Humans validated the human project by entry into the universe project. Ritual integrates us into the universe project particularly at the moments of transition: transition from winter quietness to the calmness of springtime or fullness of summer; the autumn harvest into the winter quiet. There are ritual celebrations in each season of the year, and there are ritual celebrations at dawn and at sunset of each day. The day and the season cycles are the two dominant cycles of the natural world that control the human world.

So basically we're all here for the same reason – the plants, the animals, the humans.

Berry: Everything is here for the same reason, for manifestation and celebration. But the humans articulate this. The others cannot articulate it reflectively. They can be a manifestation but they cannot reflect on that. Humans can, therefore our role is to be spokespersons for the universe and to appreciate the universe as the context in which the Divine and human meet.

So we're the earth reflecting on itself?

Berry: We are the Earth reflecting, and the Earth reflects on itself in us.

The Mind Of God: The Scientific Basis for a Rational World

– BY –

Paul Davies

Let us now return to the theological analogue. This mixture of contingency and necessity corresponds to a God who necessarily determines what alternative worlds are available to nature, but who leaves open the freedom of nature to choose from among the alternatives. In process theology the assumption is made that the alternatives are necessarily fixed in order to achieve a valued end result, i.e., they direct or encourage the (otherwise unconstrained) universe to evolve toward something good. Yet within this directed framework there remains openness. The world is therefore neither wholly determined nor arbitrary but, like Wheeler's cloud, an intimate amalgam of chance and choice.

We are barred from ultimate knowledge, from ultimate explanation, by the very rules of reasoning that prompt us to seek such an explanation in the first place. If we wish to progress beyond, we have to embrace a different concept of "understanding" from that of rational explanation. Possibly the mystical path is a way to such an understanding. I have never had a mystical experience myself, but I keep an open mind about the value of such experiences. Maybe they provide the only route beyond the limits to which science and philosophy can take us, the only possible path to the Ultimate.

The central theme that I have explored in this book is that, through science, we human beings are able to grasp at least some of nature's secrets. We have cracked part of the cosmic code. Why this should be, just why *Homo sapiens* should carry the spark of rationality that provides the key to the universe, is a deep enigma. We, who are children of the universe – animated stardust – can nevertheless reflect on the nature of that same universe, even to the extent of glimpsing the rules on which it runs. How we have become linked into this cosmic dimension is a mystery. Yet the linkage cannot be denied.

What does it mean? What is Man that we might be party to such privilege? I cannot believe that our existence in this universe is a mere quirk of fate, an accident of history, an incidental blip in the great cosmic drama. Our involvement is too intimate. The physical species *Homo* may count for nothing, but the existence of mind in some organism on some planet in the universe is surely a fact of fundamental significance. Through conscious beings the universe has generated self-awareness. This can be no trivial detail, no minor byproduct of mindless, purposeless forces. We are truly meant to be here.

Excerpted from *The Mind of God: The Scientific Basis for a Rational World* (New York: Simon & Schuster, 1992), pp. 184–185, 231–32.

Stalking Natural Spirit:
A Communion of Selves

– BY –

Bill Cahalan

All things, not just "our" selves are selves—ceaselessly self-organizing and in the process both differentiating from and communing with each other and with the larger selves which contain them. Everything, including ourselves, is interwoven with everything else, constantly receiving from, giving to, and ultimately transforming into other beings and elements.

Each self is contained within progressively larger selves—atoms within molecules within cells within people. Even a "gathered meeting" of humans may be seen as a self. And people interwoven with other animals, plants, all other living beings and the elements constitute the Earth as a self, as a body within which we are "cells." And Earth's solar system belongs to the Milky Way galaxy within the Virgo Supercluster of galaxies. And all of these self-organizing beings are the temporary expression of the ultimate, enduring Self, the Cosmos.

Earth, as such a self, has for more than three billion years evolved an ongoing increase in complexity. This has included an increasing diversity of living beings, as well as increasingly complex natural communities com-

182

posed of these beings in predominantly cooperative relationships with each other. However, human activity is
now bringing about Earth's sixth major extinction
spasm, having ended the Cenezoic era, the greatest flowering of diversity in Earth's history. This is perhaps the
greatest tragedy of our global ecological crisis.

The web of life evolved from "non-living" matter which
nonetheless embodies "organizing intelligence." We are
composed of the elements within soil, water, air and light,
and return parts of ourselves and eventually all of ourselves to these elements. The entire living web, or biosphere,
is not only formed from these elements, but also has
shaped the composition of soil, water, and air, and actively
maintains them in what would otherwise be a state of
disequilibrium. Life keeps these elements in the kind of
dynamic state necessary for life to continue. For example,
the oxygen content of the air has never been outside the
range of 15 percent to 25 percent which has allowed life
to exist continuously for 3.8 billion years. Without active
maintenance by the web of life, oxygen would never have
reached a significant level or, if it had, it would have decreased
to a very low level again by merging with certain other
elements, as is its natural tendency.

The elements which compose us are forms which the
light of the original Flaring Forth has taken. And we not
only come from and will return to, but also help the web
of life to maintain these elements, forms of light, which
compose us and contain us. Is this not a revelation of
great mystery and beauty? Might it not help radically
transform how we experience ourselves and our fellow
beings within nature's body, within the wind, the rain,
and the very landscape and sky?

Nature Tries Anything
That Works

– AN INTERVIEW WITH –

Edgar Mitchell

What do you see as the reason that we as humans are on this planet?

Mitchell: Let me give you a sentence: It would appear from a quantum cosmology that nature, in its self-organization, has used and is using every possible combination of energy to create any and all possible combinations of physical form and those that fit into a particular environmental niche. Those that flourish continue to grow and evolve. Let me give you an example: In the last few years we have gone to the deepest part of the Mariana Trench and looked at sea life there that totally blew people away. It is totally amazing, all shapes, sizes, colors, camouflage markings, eyeballs on the end of probes, feet, fins, in every possible configuration, suggesting that nature in a given environment tries anything that works. And if it works, it continues to flourish. If it doesn't work out, it dies out. It doesn't fit that niche. That seems to be the process at work here. We intelligent (so-called) human beings, *homo sapiens* evolved, flourished and grew because it was an inevitable evolution of complexity and we happened to be in an environmental niche in which we can survive and keep going. Now we have evolved to the state of consciousness where our choices are essential. Evolution is coming under conscious control at this point and if we don't wise up our bad choices are going to terminate Earth's evolution. That seems to be, in my cosmology, how you explain what's happening.

Honor the Body as Sacred

– BY –

Ron Bohannon

Human Beings have a unique sense of Freedom,
as we have the freedom to do whatever we want or choose.
This is a very simple way to operate within the Universe,
which is extremely clear about the options available to us.
We have been given this wonderful gift of the Freedom
of Choice,
  which ultimately allows us to do anything that we desire,
  as long as it does not bring pain upon another person.

Human Beings were birthed of water and clay from the Earth,
  being composed of the elements from the soil, air and water.
  Thus the Earth brought us into being from an Expanding Universe;
  whereby, we are empowered as the Living Consciousness
of the Earth.
  Gaia chose to give us life, while sustaining our existence
on the surface,
  but this process was meant to be complimentary and
not a one-sided usury.

With the advent of the multitude of all the different mechanization processes,

We become dis-membered from the very core of our unique existence on Earth.

With the multitude of technical advances that have come along for easier living,

we have become disenchanted with our very own existence and usefulness to God.

We have lost our unique connection with the Earth as our source of empowerment,

As we have discontinued the rituals and practices that united us with Earth Mother.

We continue to distance ourselves from our Spirituality and our Divine Roots,

when we fail to maintain the rituals and practices that keep us connected to Gaia.

The pain of living that we continue to feel in our existence on a regular basis,

we have been conditioned to accept as natural, but is not really normal,

only the result of our disconnection and dis-memberment from the Earth.

As we allow our Heart, Mind, Body and Soul to come into Balance,

then we begin to fully live spontaneously, instead of controlling life.

Slowly, we begin to release the need to analyze before we interact,

allowing our thought processes to develop into an automatic response, in combination with all the desires of our Heart, Mind, Body and Soul.

We have often been told that it is a sin to recognize our connection to God.

Over and over, we have been told it is wrong to live out our own Divinity,

yet we have also been chastised that it is wrong to live out our Humanity.

We simply need to recognize that we already possess all that we desire !

Ritual – Honor the Body as Sacred:

The following ritual should help us to connect,
As we identify the sacredness of the human body.
This Ritual is designed to honor the human body,
Connecting us with our unique physical qualities.

Give worship and praise to our Loving Creator God,
Which allows this reward to be received upon ourselves:

Creator God,
Anoint us with the Everlasting Waters of Joy and Gratitude.

Creator God,
Allow us to become open in our Heart, Soul, Mind and Body.

Creator God,
Let us be open and willing to freely receive the blessings given to us.

For greater effect in receiving this ritual,
It should be spoken out loud to the Universe.
This ritual can be performed with movement,
Which can be done either in a group or alone.

We have been given a Body,
which possesses Sacred Gifts to share.

We have been given Sacred Eyes,
where all we See becomes Holy!

We have been given Sacred Ears,
where all we Hear becomes Holy!

We have been given Sacred Mouths,
where all we Speak becomes Holy!

We have been given Sacred Hands,
where all we Touch becomes Holy!

We have been given Sacred Minds,
where all we Know becomes Holy!

We have been given Sacred Hearts,
where all we LOVE becomes Holy!

We have been given Sacred Souls,
where all within the Spirit is Holy!

We are part of the Sacred Universe,
where we Realize that we are Holy!!!.

An Address at
the Art Institute in Chicago

– BY –
Matthew Fox

...Cosmology I think is three things. First, it is a creation story we get from our elders. In the West this means from our scientists. And this is what is coming alive today. This is why so many scientists today are mystics again. A second dimension of cosmology is the awe and wonder; therefore the mystical experience we undergo in responding to a creation story. The third dimension of cosmology is art. It is those members of a community that can put into color and dance and song and story – this awe and this origin story. When you have those three elements working together – science, mysticism, and art – you have cosmology, and this is the great news of our time – that we are being gifted with a new cosmology at this very moment in history when we need it so desperately. Thomas Berry says "ecology is functional cosmology." Or to put it differently, ecology is the localizing of the cosmological awareness, and of how our wonder and our responsibility is intricately connected to our relationship to nature and the universe all around us.

Excerpted from *Creation Spirituality Network Magazine*, Vol. 12, #1, Spring 1996.

Consciousness:
Evolution's New Edge

– BY –
Peter Russell

Science finds it difficult to deal with consciousness at the moment because it's the one thing that doesn't fit into the current scientific worldview. There's nothing that predicts that any living being should have an inner world of experience. Yet the fact that we are experiencing beings is the one thing that we are absolutely clear on.

At the moment, science is trying to explain consciousness in terms of the material reality; it asks how consciousness emerges from the world of space, time and matter. I believe that for science to really understand consciousness, it will have to make a radical shift in worldview. In the end, it is going to have to accept that consciousness is absolutely fundamental to the universe. When it does so, it's going to find itself opening up to a whole new understanding of what spirituality is about. And when I say "Spirituality" I am not talking about religion, but the kind of experiences reported by the mystics who've explored the depths of their own consciousness. This to me is what spiritual exploration is all about – the direct firsthand exploration of the human mind.

Excerpted from *Earthlight*, Fall 1999.

Ecofeminism
and Panentheism

– AN INTERVIEW WITH –
Ivone Gebara

...what you call" holistic ecofeminism," the third phase, would it offer a new anthropology and cosmology for Christianity?

GEBARA:...Holistic ecofeminism questions a theology that sees God as above all things. God has always been used by both the left and the right to justify particular political programs. There simply is no pure God.

There is also a growing suspicion that the age-old conviction that "redemption comes through suffering" might not be true. There is growing dissatisfaction with liberation theology. The promise of a new society founded upon justice and equality just hasn't happened. We are tired of the struggle, which is often violated and which promises our liberation at the end. All we have seen is destruction and death, never victory. So we are suspicious of this approach, tired of yet another document. Analysis on the political and economic situation of our people is very important, but it is not everything!

Instead, we look at the air, the water, the Earth. We look at all the garbage surrounding us, and we sense deep within ourselves that our planet is not just a place—it is our own body. Ecofeminism proposes a new relationship with the Earth and with the entire cosmos.

For me, "holistic ecofeminism" has a double purpose. First is the fundamental concern for the oppressed—the voiceless of history—who when they are born are de facto excluded from the chance to live full lives because of their economic situation. It is the poor who are the greatest consumers of patriarchal religion because of the consolation it provides! They are caught in a vicious circle here, but for me it is absolutely key to avoid distancing myself from these voiceless ones. Second is the commitment to put an end to patriarchy in all its forms.

But what are you proposing when you say we must change the anthropological basis upon which Christianity is built?

GEBARA: I suggest that we must first change our image of men and women within the cosmos. And when we change that image, our image of God changes. Any image of God is nothing more than the image of the experience or the understanding we have of ourselves. We must re-situate the human within - not above - the cosmos. This is diametrically opposed to a Christian anthropology that insists humanity is "lord of creation" ordered by the Creator to "increase and dominate the Earth." In the current anthropology, the human's right to dominate, control, and possess has been legitimatized by the Creator and thus becomes part of human nature, pre-established - and therefore impossible to change.

We must break with our dualistic constructs of God and of the world – constructs that are hierarchical and tend to exclude the "other" as less valuable; for example, God is separated from the world; man from woman; heaven from Earth; good from bad. If one is good, one cannot be bad; if one is master, one cannot be a slave, and so on.

Yet I am convinced that this way of thinking is shifting. Today we are beginning to experience who we are in a different way – more holistically. Why? Because we are beginning to suffer because our water is dirty, our rivers and oceans are dirty, because our food isn't very good anymore. We feel great pain at such destruction. We sense at a gut level that we too are "dirty," somehow "polluted" as well. Our intuition tells us what many so-called primitive peoples have already held: that we are all in all.

The scientists are also showing us how our very "power over" is tragic because it is not only causing our own destruction as human beings, but it is destroying life itself! We humans cannot live if we destroy the rest of our body.

And so we are beginning to discover our interconnectedness. We humans are not "lords of creation." Instead, we are the Earth's thought, the Earth's reflection of itself; one type of consciousness present on the planet.

Therefore, when we behold the sick body of the poor, and see the injustice they suffer, we see it as our own body. There is no other. The other is myself. We are part of one immense, pulsating body that has been evolving for billions of years – and is still evolving.

Excerpted from "Cosmic Theology, Ecofeminism and Pantheism," *Creation Spirituality*, November/December 1993.

Cosmogenesis

– BY –

Stephan Snider, Omar Zinn and Drew Dellinger

The universe is in a continuous process of meta-
morphosis
constantly changing, constantly evolving
into an evermore complex and differentiated reality.
Baby within Mother, Mother within Earth
Earth within a time/developmental universe.
As we look into this nebulous spacious place
that our race of human beings is seeing
We see consciousness expanding
look up from where you're standin'
to embrace this crazy place that God creates
The creator creates the creation
the relationship is a direct connection
and in your eye is the divine reflection
so check it out...and look again
'cause the flame has lit up the world from within
So get into this synthesis, harmonious consciousness
in tune with this marvelous, miraculous, wondrous
universe
Infinite, infinitesimal, infinite but inexpressible
I'm just a man, a cosmic decimal

but in my mind I hold all things together
For ever and ever and ever and ever
19 billion years behind me, chillin' inside me
always remindin' me.

"Cosmogenesis," *Creation Spirituality Network*, Vol. 12,
#2, Summer 1996.

Cyberspace and the Dream of Teilhard de Chardin

– BY –

John R. Mabry

...We have reached the end of the expanding, or "diversity" stage, and are now entering the contracting, or "unifying" stage. At this point, Chardin's theory runs completely counter to Darwin's, in that the success of humanity's evolution in the second stage will not be determined by "survival of the fittest," but by our own capacity to converge and unify. The most important initial evolutionary leap of the convergence stage is the formation of what Chardin termed "the Noosphere." Its formation, as Michael Murray explains, begins with "a global network of trade, communications, accumulation, and exchange of knowledge, cooperative research...all go into the weaving of the material support for a sphere of collective thought. In the field of science alone, no individual knows more than a tiny fraction of the sum of scientific knowledge, and each scientist is dependent not only for his education but for all his subsequent work on the traditions and resources which are the collective possession of an entire international society composed of the living and the dead. Just as Earth once covered itself with a film of interdependent living organisms which we call the bio-

sphere, so mankind's combined achievements are form-
ing a global network of collective minds."

"The idea," writes Chardin, "is that of the Earth not
only covered by myriads of grains of thought, but enclosed in a single thinking envelope so as to form a single
vast grain of thoughts on the sidereal scale, the plurality
of individual reflections grouping themselves together
and reinforcing one another in the act of a single unani-
mous reflection." One hesitates to invoke the terms
"group-mind" or "hive mentality," but they are, perhaps,
leaps made by far less developed creatures than we that
presage our own assent. We know that such a thing can
and does exist in a variety of species, especially ants, mi-
gratory birds, and others....

Chardin waxes poetic (as he often does) when he describes it: "Noosphere...the living membrane which is
stretched like a film over the lustrous surface of the star
which holds us. An ultimate envelope taking on its own
individuality and gradually detaching itself like a luminous aura. This envelope was not only conscious, but
think...the Very Soul of the Earth." Not only are our
bodies the stuff of the Earth's body, but our minds are
the consciousness of this being, the Earth. We have supposed that we are individuals, but we "are dust, and to
dust ye shall return." We have supposed our minds are
our own, that even if the Earth is conscious of herself in
us, she is conscious of being many little selves; but perhaps, as theorists in the field of transpersonal psychology suggest, we are mistaken. Chardin, in fact, argues
that it must be so, that "what we are aware of is only the
nucleus which is ourselves. The interaction of souls
would be incomprehensible if some 'aura' did not extend

from one to the other, something proper to each one and common to all." Chardin believes, too, that this consciousness is not only psychological, but of the greatest spiritual importance, as well. "Nothing is precious," he says, "except that part of you which is in other people, and that part of others which is in you. Up there, on high, everything is one."

How is it that such an awesome phenomenon could possibly come to be? Amazingly, Teilhard predicts the evolution of a machine that hardly even existed in his time beyond being a glorified abacus: the computer. "Here I am thinking," he writes in *Man's Place in Nature*, "of those astonishing electronic machines (the starting-point and hope of the young science of cybernetics), by which our mental capacity to calculate and combine is reinforced and multiplied by a process and to a degree that heralds as astonishing advances in this direction as those that optical science has already produced for our power of vision." Teilhard's vision of what computers would do for us is twofold. First, the computers will achieve the completion of our brains, in that there would be the instantaneous retrieval of information around the globe. Second, computers will improve our brains by facilitating processes more quickly than our own resources can achieve them.

It is also interesting that Chardin predicted the use of the prefix "cyber" in regards to the computer/human matrix, since "cyber" is all the rage in computering circles. In fact, what can be seen as the progenitor of Teilhard's Noosphere is now being termed "Cyberspace" by the computer press, in reference to that mystical field of interconnected computer pathways wherein all of the exchanges are made. As Michael Benedikt describes it in his *Collected Abstracts from the First Conference on Cyberspace*, "Cyberspace is a globally networked, computer-sustained, computer-accessed, and computer-generated, multi-dimensional, artificial, or 'virtual' reality. In this world, onto which every computer screen is a window, actual, geographical distance is irrelevant. Objects seen or heard are neither physical nor necessarily presentations of physical objects, but are rather – in form, character, and action – made up of data, of pure information. This information is derived in part from the operation of the natural, physical world, but derived primarily from the immense traffic of symbolic information, images, sounds and people, that constitute human enterprise in science, art, business and culture."

The form most of the exchanges take is the computer "bulletin board." On this, any person with the simplest of computers and a modem can call a central, master computer with which literally any number of other users may be linked. Once connected, a person may receive or distribute messages on any given topic to one or a million people. As John Barlow describes it, "In this silent world, all conversation is typed. To enter it, one forsakes both body and place and becomes a thing of words alone. You can see what your neighbors are saying (or recently said), but not what either they or their physical surroundings look like. Town meetings are continuous and discussions range on everything from sexual kinks to depreciation schedules" ("Trouble in Cyberspace," *The Humanist* Sept/Oct 1991)...

In light of developments such as computer bulletin boards and "super-information highways" like the Internet, Teilhard's fantastic notions don't seem so fantastic. He is, it turns out, the unsung prophet of our collective future. It is time that we begin to look forward to what these developments are going to mean to us personally, developmentally. Chardin says that, "Humankind is now caught up, as though in a train of gears, at the heart of a continually accelerating vortex of self-totalization." We need to consider how the inevitable changes in our nature are going to affect us as individuals – spiritually, psychologically, and pathologically. One advantage, though, to facing what is happening to us is that we can stop "groping about" in the dark, and take conscious control of our evolution to speed it on its way.

We are therefore, in the latter twentieth century, at the threshold of another great leap in evolution, the contraction and unification of the human species, the construction of the Noosphere, the focusing of our psychic energies. "The powers that we have released," Chardin states in *Human Energy*, "could not possibly be absorbed by the narrow system of individual or national units which the architect of the human Earth have hitherto used. *The age of nations has passed. Now unless we wish to perish we must shake off our old prejudices and build the Earth.*" (Italics mine.) How we accomplish this is by correcting our errant perception of reality as being made up of separate units. Chardin insists that "to love is to discover and complete one's self in someone other than oneself, an act impossible of general realization on Earth so long as each can see in the neighbor no more than a close fragment following its own course through the world. It is precisely this state of isolation that will end if we begin to discover in each other not merely the elements of one and the same thing, but of a single Spirit in search of itself."

The result of such a realization is the Noosphere, toward which we are moving even now, via our cybernetic interconnections, know it or not, like it or not, want it or not. As our consciousness of unity progresses, the standard of morality will eventually not be placed on the maintenance of private property, but upon the health of the Whole, which will become more and more perceptible to us as Noogenesis unfolds. Chardin himself admits that "these perspectives will appear absurd to those who don't see that life is, from its origins, groping, adventurous, and dangerous. But these perspectives will grow, like an irresistible idea on the horizon of new generations." Indeed, it seems less and less absurd as this very process unfolds before us.

Excerpted from *Creation Spirituality*, Summer 1994, pp. 23–26.

PART THREE
Where Are We Going?

Community of Life   © 2001 by Marian C. Honors, OSB

Where Are We Going?

– BY –

Catherine Browning

Where are we going?
Deliver us a line.
About the journey to be taken,
Into future realms of time.

Are we going to heaven or Hades,
Are we going body and soul,
Are we going for apocalypse,
Or trusting evolution's flow?

Weave a tale for us,
Spin a metaphor or two,
About the grandeur of Mystery,
In a cosmos vast and true.

In the third quarter of life, looking into the shadows of my fourth quarter, the notion of death is becoming more present. In earlier years, life was here now and in the future, with death being not much more than a philosophical concept. No one of close acquaintance died until I was in my late 20's. Since then, the deaths of my mother, father, in-laws, and friends have brought the reality of death into my awareness.

Except for a few years of depression in my early 20's, a few dark nights of the soul, and some minor physical ailments, my life has been good. I have been blessed with a belief in the Earth and universe, and in humans and other species, which has made every day of my life a joyful, exciting, and mysterious blessing. It would seem, therefore, that I should look into what a blessed death looks like, after living a blessed life.

It would seem that a blessed life and a blessed death require a sense of deep appreciation of an Earth that has been very gracious. However, being alive is a known; death is an unknown. The deaths of the many people and other creatures I have known, by their very nature, have prevented them from sharing the experience of dying with me. People write much about their experience of living, but only through their supposition of death. We know the heart stops beating, the lungs stop breathing, and the brain no longer functions. But the age-old question still begs for an answer: "Is this the end? Or do we, in some form, continue?" Of all the death questions, this seems to be the most profound and personal, and it may be the question that sparks all the other ultimate questions.

As a Catholic, the answers were very clear to me. If I obeyed the rules, avoided sin, and communicated with God, I would end up in heaven. This was the whole purpose of life. Opportunities to do sinful things surrounded me, day in and day out, so it was important to be ever vigilant. And when I died, there would be eternal life after death. The only question was where I would be experiencing eternity – heaven or hell.

The new cosmology that opened a whole new dimension of who God is, a lack of deep appreciation for and celebration of the Earth, and my revelations on the divine purpose of man began to change all of my beliefs, including those that centered on an afterlife. Having concluded that the dogma of my religion was and is leading to the destruction of the Earth, I opened to a new cosmology, and new answers to the question of what happens after death.

As I write this, it is clear to me that I do not have the answer. I find the ideas and thoughts in the following chapter to be thought-provoking and hopeful...and they provide me with a sense of comfort in not knowing the answer. My appreciation and respect for this magnificent Earth, and the blessing of being alive here and now, bring a sense of gratitude and peace within me, knowing that whatever happens when I die will be good, and will be as it should be.

CHAPTER FIVE
Where Are We Going:
A Personal Perspective

Death: A Tremendous Mystery

– BY –

Miriam Therese MacGillis

I still see death as such a tremendous mystery. A number of years ago I heard Thomas Berry reflect on death. What he said touched me deeply. He said, "we cannot die out of the universe, we can only die in, there is no way to leave it." This statement opened up something very powerful in me.

I don't know what death will be like, but I trust it. I trust that we cannot leave. I believe I carry the whole mystery and consciousness of the universe and it is focused in me right now. I am evolving, as it is evolving. Universe is evolving, and I am not separate. Thomas Berry says we have our small selves and our large selves and when we die, our small self returns to its large self. The small self is just the vehicle in which the large self is existing and actually participating in the great work of creation. I really believe that I am involved in the creation of the outer and the inner structure of the universe. In my little, feeble, limited way of understanding, I believe it is what each of us is doing. I want to participate in a way that brings the whole into a deeper love and communion. When I die, I'll just let go of this set of molecules. Somehow, I'm not afraid of letting go the way

I used to be. My sense of already being connected to something larger allows me to trust. I don't know what it is going to be like, I just trust it.

I have accompanied a number of people to the doorway of death. I have experienced my participation in their death as a high honor and privilege. I know it is partially because of the people themselves. Their dying was like a glow going out of a candle. When you put a glass over a candle, it slowly runs out of oxygen and just fades. That is how I have seen people die, as a gentle fading. My sense is that people hear until the very end at a deep inner level of consciousness. Even at a comatose level, a person hears and accepts what is said. It is important to tell the dying how good they are, to remind them of the good they did for others, what a blessing their life has been and how you are going to carry their spirit and memory forward.

There was a Dominican sister who had deeply studied and pondered the universe story before her death. She and everyone around her experienced her dying in this context. She just moved into death consciously, without fear, like an adventure. She entered freely. That is the way I want to die, too, as a new phase in my journey. What are we worried about? The life, death, rebirth process has been integral to the universe and Earth for billions of years. Nothing is lost, just transformed.

I find a consolation in rethinking death, which appears to be such an ultimate separation. But separation is just a human perception, defined by the limitations of our sensing organs. The New Story sheds such a different light, for we know beyond a shadow of a doubt that the universe is a single interacting unity, which is why we can't leave it. So, even the impression that death is a separation is just a human construct, a belief based on our limited perceptions. Death is a word we invented to describe a phenomenon we were experiencing with our eyes, ears, and senses. It isn't what we think it is. There is no such thing as death – it is just a word for the phenomena that is going on every moment, everywhere in the universe. It is a form of change.

Throughout history, people could only imagine what death meant and construct meanings around it, like immortality, resurrection or reincarnation. It is still a mystery, like, "Why is there a universe?" Basically we are describing the ponderings of our species which is very, very young, just recently evolved.

Life after death is about change. I think of it as the ongoing dynamics of chaos and complexity as described by physicists. What we call death and what we call resurrection are not one-time events. They describe the way the universe works. Resurrection is the ongoing emergence of every moment. I can't even hold in my conscious mind what is going on right now in my body, or inside my room. Molecules and atoms are exchanging place at the speed of light.

Thomas Berry says everything is in a perpetual state of exodus. I have always understood the exodus as a one-time historic event in the life of Israel. In this new understanding exodus becomes a condition for existence. In human existence it is multilayered, a process of constantly leaving one's self behind in order to bring forth what is not yet actualized. Humans begin participating consciously, freely, in what the universe and Earth have been doing forever. My small self and great self are always in exodus. They are always leaving what they are in any given moment, going into chaos in order to re-emerge transformed.

Hidden Life: Conversing With a Child About Death

– BY –

Kym Farmer

The weight on my heart was as tangible as a stone. I sat next to Laura and watched her turn the egg I had given her over and over in her hand, softly stroking with her other hand the feathers of the little yellow chick nestled in the crumpled front of her dress. We were on the back porch of her grandmother's familiar farmhouse – my Aunt Edna's – while the adults inside murmured at her wake. I had led her outside after I found her bewildered eyes locked on mine in the crush of people inside.

Most of us adults have heard the sentiment expressed that it is so difficult to experience a child dying before we do. It just doesn't seem to be in the natural order of things. And yet it is also difficult for us adults to try to respond effectively to a child when things *do* occur in the natural order – when an older person dies and a child must experience that loss. We may commiserate with hugs and attention, but we frequently feel at a loss as to how to help the child express her feeling. The child is not likely to have the words (literally) to explain – even to herself – all the feelings that are rolling around at an emotional time such as this. How can we help?

For most of humanity, death is a spiritual experience in one way or another. Regardless of whether or not we have a concept of an afterlife, death itself is steeped in mystery. Not only do we not know with certainty what comes next, but death invites us to reflect, consciously or not, on why we're here at all – what does it mean to experience this time, if we are going to die in the end anyway? In what context does the reality of death have significance? We may not be able to ponder concepts this deep with young children, but if we are going to talk with them at all about death, it's best to recognize from the get-go that we are in a spiritual context.

How, then, do we connect the known with the Unknown? How do we bridge between a reality far more concrete than a child might like and an abstract with which most of us adults grapple? I have found that the clearest examples that leap to mind in such circumstances are those from the natural world. This fact in itself is very telling. We are so profoundly and so intimately connected with the natural world, with its deep mysteries and life lessons, that we instinctually and immediately turn there when looking for ways to express numinous reality. And, as it turns out, the natural world is ready with countless expressions – out-picturings – of the meaningful truths we seek to access. As we continue to interact with the child over the months of the mourning process, we can pull one or another of these ideas out of our pockets as timely treasures when the child's heart needs them most.

In my experience with Laura, I might summarize our ongoing conversations over time as something like this: "I know this has been such a sad time for you, Laura, since your Grandma died. I felt the same way when my own grandmother died. I missed her so much.

"One of the things we used to do often was take walks in the park. There was always so much happening there, and we never ran out of things to do – butterflies to chase, trees to climb, leaves to match, bird feathers to tickle each other with, flowers to smell, drawings to make from shadows, and usually a sunset to watch before we walked home. I used to bring home some of these treasures and keep them in a special box in my room. I would take them out and look at them, and just doing that would remind me so clearly of our time together. I still have that box. I brought it with me today, because I wanted to show you some things in it.

"This leaf came from that big old oak tree in the center of the park. I loved the way the outlines of the veins remained even after the rest of the leaf decayed. It looks like such a fragile delicate thing, and yet it has lasted so long. I picked it up from the ground one fall afternoon. Have you ever seen one like it? Not all of the leaves were off the trees yet, but I knew they were going to be because winter was coming. And every winter, all those trees in the park lose their leaves. They look so lifeless during the winter, don't they? Like there's just not a breath of life left inside them. And yet, every spring, those trees that look like big dead sticks show us that they still have all that new life hiding in them – they send out *millions* of new leaves!

"This little blue eggshell is from a hatched baby robin. You can see how it almost fits together perfectly. When it's just an eggshell like this, it's hard to imagine that there's all this life going on inside, isn't it? Just like that egg and chick in your lap. Over all those weeks, that baby bird was bringing itself into being, and from the outside, we couldn't tell a thing - it looked as still as a stone.

"Here's a bulb from some purple irises that my Grandma and I planted one day underneath the maple by the birdbath. This looks a lot like that eggshell in a way, doesn't it? Seems like nothing is going on inside, and yet every spring we would go back and see those irises pushing up again, sending out a brand new flower from a bulb that looked like this! One year I pressed one of the flowers in a book and saved it in my box, too. Here's what it looks like. So beautiful, isn't it?

"This is something you've probably seen before. The cocoon on this twig is for a monarch butterfly. The twig broke off and fell to the ground, and the cocoon got stepped on a little bit, but I saved it anyway. You know, a lot of people think that a caterpillar makes a cocoon that it goes into, where it snoozes for a time while it grows wings, then comes out later as a butterfly. But what *really* happens is even more of a miracle: After the caterpillar builds its cocoon around itself, everything that was the caterpillar dissolves. Then, in some mysterious way, the wisdom still inside that cocoon reorganizes itself and puts itself back together as a butterfly! When it comes out, it's really a whole different creature than the caterpillar, and even more beautiful. Imagine that! Think about what you would be like if *you* did that - and came out even more beautiful than you are!

"Here are a couple of drawings Gramma and I did together. We traced around shadows on the ground. I thought the shadow looked like a duck, so that's what I made mine into - see? But she thought it looked like a rabbit - so here's what she made it into. The shadows would get longer as the sun went down, and change their shapes. So we would finally stop exploring, and sit down on a bench to watch the sun set. It's really such a splendid sight, even though it means that darkness is coming. Do you ever worry about the dark? But every morning when you get up – there's the sun again.

"Death is kind of like that, too. Everything seems dark for a while – it's almost like the sun has vanished. But it hasn't really, has it – it's just out of our sight for a while. Like the life of the flower that's in the bulb which we can't see; like the life of the bird that's in the egg which we can't see; like the life of the leaves that hide within the tree when it's so bare in winter.

"That life does not go away. But like the caterpillar, the shape it had dissolves – into something even more lovely. This is a strange and marvelous and mysterious thing. But we can look all around us in the rest of God's world and know that this is so. As true as it is for the egg and for the bulb and for the cocoon and for the tree and for the sun – it's true also for your Grandma. She has changed in a way that we can't recognize any more, but she has become something even more beautiful. And even though your Grandma can't speak to you any more in the ways that she used to, I think that she – and all the other beings who have died – speak to us with stories from the egg and the bulb and the cocoon and the sun. It's the same way God speaks.

"I'm going to leave this box with you so that you can begin to collect your own reminders of your Grandma. And maybe you'll come from time to time to show me what *you* have found that reminds you of how your Grandma was with you, and how she still can be."

Death

– BY –

Michael Dowd

Growing up Roman Catholic, as a child I was taught that death for all other creatures meant the absolute end. But death for human beings brought one of three possibilities: heaven (if you were good), hell (if you were bad), or purgatory (if you were mostly good but did a few bad things).

As a teenager and young adult, after my born again experience and conversion to Protestant Pentecostalism, I still understood what happens at (or after) death pretty much the same way, although I dropped my belief in purgatory. Fundamentally, I saw heaven and hell as literal places. When someone died, that person's soul (their true essence) went to one place or the other, depending on whether or not they had been saved – that is, whether or not they had accepted Jesus Christ as their personal Lord and Savior. Heaven was paradise: mansions of gold, no crying, dying, or hardship. I imagined everyone in heaven praising God all day long – a never-ending worship service with music, liturgical dancing, and beautiful (albeit sexless) angels. I imagined hell, on the other hand, as absolute torment. Damnation in a lake of fire. Eternal separation from God. Never-ending pain and suffering; weeping and gnashing of teeth. Of course, since I imagined heaven and hell as actual places, I also imagined them in spatial terms: heaven was up (in the heavens), hell was down (where lava comes from, I suppose; I never thought about it deeply because I knew that I wasn't going there!).

Now that I embrace an evolutionary view of the universe, I understand heaven and hell symbolically, mythically. I see heaven as the experience of being consciously aware of my true Nature and living out of the heart space of love, trust, and gratitude. I experience heaven to the degree that I trust the universe, follow my heart, and am a channel of divine grace and creative evolutionary power in the world.

I see hell as the experience of being mentally separated from reality – being caught up in fear, cynicism, distrust, selfishness, bitterness, illusion, falsity, hatred, or anything else that keeps me alienated from love. To be *in* hell is to be a cell in the body without knowing it, like a cancer cell, and thus cut off from my true self, my true nature. To be *in* heaven is to be aware of my identity as a cell in the divine body, and to allow the will and purpose of the larger self of the universe, God, to flow naturally and effortlessly through me.

Heaven and hell have thus transformed into states of being for me in *this* life. Death itself has taken on new meaning as well. I am less concerned with what death is than in how I wish to *be* when the time draws near. I wish to be ready for death, accepting of death, even jubilant of death as the final letting go of all illusion and attachment. Prepared for death, I will surrender into the Great Mystery.

I know that the atoms and molecules of my body shall return to Earth to nourish and sustain others; I fervently hope that I shall have lived my life such that my actions and contributions will also. But what of my spirit, my soul? Here, a story tells it best.

During the process of my becoming a United Church of Christ minister, in the late 1980s, I presented and defended my ordination paper to a gathering of ministers and lay leaders in western Massachusetts. After my presentation, entitled "A Deep Ecology Perspective on the UCC Statement of Faith," during the question-and-answer period, a well-respected minister stood up and said, "Michael, I'm quite impressed with your presentation, and with this evolutionary theology you've shared with us. However, the little boy in me wants to know: Where is Emory?" Emory Wallace, a well-known and widely beloved retired minister who had had been my mentor, had died suddenly, just a few weeks before this ordination hearing. This was my response:

"In order to answer that question I have to use both day language – the language of rational, everyday discourse – and night language – the language of dreams and symbols and myths. Both types of speech are vital and necessary, just as both states of consciousness are vital and necessary. As I'm sure you know, if we are deprived of the opportunity to dream for any length of time – as mammals, as primates, as humans – we die. But, of course, we fully understand and accept that day language and night language are very different. For example, if you were to ask me how my day went today and I were to say, 'It was great. After lunch I flew over to a nearby farm, turned into a bull, and mated with several of the cows,' and kept a straight face, you'd probably think something was very wrong with me and might suggest that perhaps a visit to the local psychiatrist might be in order. However, if you had asked me about a dream I recently had and I said the same thing, you might be curious as to the interpretation or meaning of my dream, but you wouldn't think I was losing my mind. Everyone knows that it's possible to fly or turn into another creature in the dream state.

"So in order to respond to your question, 'Where is Emory, now that he's dead?' I have to answer in two ways. First, in the language of everyday discourse, I would say, 'Emory's physical body will eventually be completely consumed by bacteria, leaving only his skeleton and teeth. His genes, contributions, and memory will continue to live on in his family and in the countless people that he touched in person and through his writings, in those they touched, and so on. And his life force or spirit - his soul - has returned to the universe, and to the Great Mystery that some of us call 'God'.

"But, you see, if I stop there, if that's all I say, then I've told only half the story. I must go on and say something like: 'And I'm sure Emory is also seated at the right hand of God the Father (or in the loving arms of God the Mother, if you prefer), surrounded by a host of heavenly angels.' And that would also be true – true within the accepted logic and understanding of night language."

Thoughts on Death

- BY -
Jim Conlon

A three-year-old child waves out the window of an air-plane, "Hi, Daddy!" He then turns to his mother and announces confidently, "My daddy is an angel, I'm talk-ing to him!" He is the son of the professional football player who died suddenly on the practice field.

An elder was asked, "Where are you going to go when you die?" His wise response was, "I'm not going anywhere."

These two incidents fly in the face of the conventional wisdom that says, "When you are dead you're gone and you either go up (heaven) or down (the other place), you certainly don't stay here.

Death is an even greater mystery than illustrated by these examples. It is ominous and foreboding because our domi-nant culture is in deep denial that it even exists. Witness how we as a society participate in "the high cost of dying" with expensive caskets, prolonged wakes and cosmetics that elicit such responses as, "Doesn't he look natural?"

It is also true that we live in a culture of death, a world where violence permeates the planet (e.g., Middle East, Ireland, Africa, Central America). In this way life is cheap and death a daily occurrence.

221

Yet for many death remains a mystery, often feared and too little understood. Perhaps you have memories from your childhood when a pet died or a recollection from an Ash Wednesday ritual when you were reminded "Remember you are dust and unto dust you will return" – experiences that only increased your confusion.

I suggest that the New Story has much to teach us; we are reminded that death is integral to existence. The cycles of the seasons, the way the seed dies so that a plant may grow, are powerful proclamations that deepen our comprehension of the mystery. From the perspective of the universe, death is a next chapter in your journey, a story of returning to your origins. It is a new chapter in your life, a transformation moment on the journey.

Shortly before his assassination, Oscar Romero proclaimed, "If they kill me, I will rise in the people of El Salvador," and he has. A friend illustrated this interconnectedness of death and rebirth when she said, "I was with my father when he died and my sister when she gave birth and the two experiences were mysteriously the same."

The story of death is that life is changed, not ended. This lesson has been revealed to us from the beginning.

Through cosmological death the galaxies were born, Earth came into being and life flourished. From the perspective of the New Story death becomes a transformative moment when we are born into a new life, a mysterious transition into a new state of existence, a communion with the divine whereby we join the great cycle of existence. In this view, the angel in a child's mind and the elder's claim for his continuing presence make sense. Rather than an ominous ending to be feared, death becomes a threshold to new life.

This Gives Me Hope

– BY –

Kelly Hicks

Three of my loved ones died within a few years of each other. The losses were amplified given the cause of death—suicide. In mourning, I was told everything from the act being a mortal sin with my loved ones remanded to hell, to their deaths being willed by some benevolent, interventionist God. These thoughts were representative of current religious belief and provided little comfort.

My family members suffered from depression, an acknowledged medical condition. Throughout our culture, a general stigma surrounds mental illness, and suicide is thought to run in families, given a strong genetic component. This explanation of neural disease is dismissed in most religious models. In fact, any kind of aberrant behavior, no matter the origin, is up for debate. How does a merciful God allow for sin and suffering?

When I first learned of a cosmology based on an evolutionary process and holy design, I experienced the first degree of comfort coping with death. Whether there was life after death, reincarnation or heavenly reward for those favored by God, no longer seemed relevant to the question of life.

The concept of an emergent universe filled with precision and grace allowed for disease, diminished DNA, and even the demise of the human species. At the same time, the story of the universe encouraged faith and trust in its abundance and elegant beauty as a sacred creative process. This gave me hope.

For beyond any existing imagery, symbol, or creation myth, I could glory in the lives of my loved ones as part of the infinite source.

Puzzling About Death

– BY –

Miriam Brown, O.P.

It's my age, I say. I find myself puzzling about death. It asks me the meaning of life and faces me with the question of God. Inside myself I find the familiar Christian prescriptions about living an upright and grateful life, being for others, an active citizen of the world. And the matching promise: readiness for "heaven," union with an awaiting God.

I long ago replaced the notion of original sin with gratitude for the blessed creation, but I am now recognizing the power of the myth of the centralness of the human – that everything is about us. We are the main characters, we tell ourselves, it is our story. Creation is given for human enjoyment and use. And even though "dominion" has shifted to "stewardship," we are still the ones in charge, responsible.

But with the mysteries of an ever-expanding universe, the youth of human culture, and my own imagination beginning to say there must surely be – now or later – conscious life in other places, I am freshly alive with wonder and curiosity. And oddly, the weight of responsibility feels lighter on my shoulders. If our ignorance and arrogance brings things to ruin here, the energy of life will not be undone. This does not make me work less hard. On the contrary, I feel privileged to participate actively in something wondrous: "a flourishing humanity on a thriving Earth in an evolving universe, all together filled with the glory of God." [1] I can see better that in our mistakes of injustice and planetary degradation, I cannot just oppose others as "them," but that our human struggles toward inclusivity and sustainability depend on our coming of age together.

The effort toward cosmic membership is a bumpy journey. I feel a new compassion and humility, the humus that assures that our special stardust belongs. Mercifully, our species too is given time to evolve. "We're on the track, we humans," wrote poet Mary Caroline Richard. And "if we're true to ourselves," we won't give up "just because we haven't got there yet." [2]

And death? That is adventure, moving into dimensions of life that "we see now only darkly." It will be a stretch, I smile broadly, learning to "breathe" in a new dimension, moving into a wider way of being connected with all that is. Meeting, in the great unfolding, the Divine "in whom we live and move and have our being." Finding through all evolving eternity (paradox) a Kindom beyond our wildest and fondest imaginings.

---

1. Elizabeth A. Johnson,CSJ, *Spiritual Questions for the Twenty-First Century*, (Orbis, Maryknoll, NY. 2001). pp. 124.

2. Mary Caroline Richards, *The Crossing Point*, (Wesleyan Press, Middletown, Connecticut, 1973). p. 184.

A Big What If

– BY –

Evonne Berube-Reiersen

if we die into Death
the great bearded white man floats
to judge our very lives
an accountant of sins
mortal and venial
parchment and pen in hand
saint peter and the archangels
as if heaven is a big party for only humans
with no vision of various life-forms
no trees
only white puffiness
music of violins
booming words through space
did we behave well enough
did we believe strongly enough
did we drag our crosses on our earthly backs
did we cry an ocean of seatears
for our injustices
for what we did not become
did we pour a river of blood
from our broken hearts

into the yearning soil of the universe's dreams
to get in or not to get in
is the agonizing question
and if not
the alternatives
raging fire an infinity of inferno black heat
the more appealing purgatory
hope salvation possibility indefinite
limbo
un-baptized babies waiting for an opportunity to
be born again
neither here nor there
No   Where

if we die into Life
the light the source the divine
into the hydrogen the stars
the rain and thunder
the not flesh
a microcosmic tornado
that cradles us in the arms of a spiral galaxy
flinging spirit into the density wave of astonish-
ing beauty
with no gates
and no hell
no tally of our deeds
that may have ruined our paradise
or claims that we created heaven while in our
bodies
intending
to do a better job of it

as if we could repair the shattering damage
of our ignorance
our longing
our joy
as if our soul
expands with the lovely cosmos
when we are sorry
when we are more
or less
conscious
returning optimistically
to continuecontinuecontinuecontinue still hope
an other form perhaps
a rock a bear a Buddha
an unidentified flying subject
in an other dimension
to exist in what is
Some   Where

if we die into Maybe
invisible fireworks exploding
a zillion quarks a gajillion strings
how many molecules does a human body contain
a spiritual supernova
spewing subatomic pieces of soul
iridescent clustering
one force
Love
manifested in the intricate intimate elemental
world
birthing the dark matter

or is the dark matter birthing a new us
pushing time   if there is such a thing
on the changing winds of hummingbirds
can we melt our desires
into solids fluids gases
into dragonflys and dolphins
spinning breath and lunar tides
tension
generously sculpting the equations
into color and multivalent being
can we freeze our torment into crystals
snowflakes amethyst diamonds glaciers pluto
infinitesimal specks of the yet immeasurable
psyche
the teeniest tiniest
wavicle
wave and particle falling into Love
that leaps the synapse of matter and spirit
touching all worlds
flowing into senses of the unseen
helping to feel
our godness harmonize
Every Where

What Happens to the Human After Death?

– BY –

Meg Hanrahan

Humans follow the same pattern of birth, life, death, and rebirth that we see enacted repeatedly in the cycles of nature on earth. At death, the spirit leaves the physical body, allowing for the transition to a new birth, into new form of some type. So we might see this as analogous to the tree dropping its leaves in the fall, and being re-cloaked in the spring; our human spirit dropping the cloak of the physical body in apparent death, to be reborn to a new form, a new life.

What a comfort this is, to know that my body will someday decompose to become one with the Earth mother and go on to nourish living species on earth in the future; meanwhile, my spirit follows new paths and new processes in the eternal dance of the universe.

Human spirits beyond death do remain connected in some way to the Earth realm and to humans still alive here. They can help effect change in the physical world though no longer in a physical body. I believe in reincarnation, the idea that individuals come back to Earth in different bodies.

We are all connected. We are all one. Life shifts and moves in a spiral dance of creation. What a gift to know myself as part of the process of love experiencing life on Earth.

(Worm)holes in the Veil

– BY –

Cherri Ann Forrest

I think about death everyday now, especially within relation to a dream I've been given to share – the dream of
our regeneration (DOOR).

My earliest recall of becoming conscious, of waking
into this life, occurred before I could walk, in the crib. I
was struck, cracked open by a powerfully lucid awareness of being, of existing, of separating self (as though I
had just popped up, like some sort of sensory mush-
room). Quietly fascinated, I gazed around the room, seeing woodwork, the windows, white roses on green wall-
paper and the animated beings that would flesh into
parents, grandparents and great grandparents. Ohhh!
(amazed) "so this is what you look like!!!"

On top of the fascination, I felt a sense of serene de-
tachment and subterranean delight. Feelings of physical
limitations or lack or impatience did not bother me. By
contrast, prior to this awakening, I simply sensed myself
as being surrounded by detail-free "warm fuzzies." The
most remarkable thing, in retrospect, was that I did not

feel like some helpless, hapless, six-month-old baby (even though I was) but more like some ageless thing, no older or younger than, say, fire.

I use my death as a tool to gage my own earthly progression: Am I on the right track? Is this in keeping with the dream? Will future kids and critters and plants coming after me be disgusted by or glad for my actions? What if I were one of those future kids? This way, I keep my process centered, and within the context of life experiences and lessons learned, I'll have no real regrets.

That my body will return to soil doesn't bother me. I love soil. I treat it reverently. It's more valuable than pure gold. And I'm fond of saying, "Earthworms make the world go round. Why else would they have five hearts???"

Death, Reborn Earth, Reborn God

– BY –

David Haenke

Earth is the God that we can know.
God is the Earth that we can know.
We come from Earth, Are Earth (each of us little
Earths),
Exist from and for Earth,
Live from Earth,
Die back to Earth and
Are re-born elementally, continuously, in and
out of forms of Earth.

Death Is More Beautiful Than We Can Imagine

– BY –

John Seed

My first thoughts of death are by Walt Whitman, where he speaks of "sweet, peaceful, welcome death."* My second thought is that my father died last year at the age of ninety eight and was cremated. I felt it took such a lot of fossil fuel to cremate my father and the worms were cheated. I made my will to have my son and Ruth bury me naked without a sheet, without a casket, without a box, with no formaldehyde or any chemicals. I want my naked body to go back to the Earth. I have taken a lot from the Earth already and I may take more before I die, so I want to give back at least a few kilos of compost. I want to feed some worms. I'm looking forward to it but am in no hurry. To me it is like going back into the miracle from which I emerged.

I am not enamored of pain. I'm not enamored of suffering. Pain and suffering often accompany the degeneration of the body and so on. I wouldn't mind dying in a painless way. It's not like I'm some kind of hero, but the death itself, I think, is going to be magnificent. It won't be magnificent for me because I'm not going to be there, I'm just going to be part of the magnificence. There are just these moments, like during the seven years of meditation when I was younger. I had two or three moments, which I imaged, were just like death. I wasn't there and nothing was there except the magnificence. I remember at one point realizing that the first thought that comes is the death of the moment. The first thought is when I disappear and all that remains is e-v-e-r-y-t-h-i-n-g. Of course there is no "I" to own this. The "I" is too small to own it anyway, that's why the "I" has to disappear. To be sentenced to e-v-e-r-y-t-h-i-n-g for eternity doesn't seem too bad to me.

---

*Walt Whitman, *Leaves of Grass and Other Selected Prose* (New York: Random House, 1950), P 42.

Death Was Not Masked, But Rather Faceless, Smooth And Unblemished

– BY –

Judith Boice, N.D., LAC

For over two years I traveled around the U.S. lecturing on menopause and women's health. Because I was constantly on the go, I carried a pager so that colleagues, friends, and family could reach me in case of emergency. My mom, unfamiliar with the technology, would call the number thinking she could reach me directly. "Mom," I told her as I returned one of her pages from an airport telephone, "I worry every time you page me. I think someone has died."

"Sorry, honey," she crooned. "I just wanted to catch up with you and find out how you're doing."

A couple of months later, I was in a hotel room in Fort Worth, Texas, preparing to have dinner with one of my co-workers. The pager next to the bed began to vibrate and flashed a familiar number: my parents in Ohio.

I dialed, remembering my last conversation about the pager with Mom. My parents sounded tense and weary when they answered.

"Ruth [my sister] was going in and out of consciousness this afternoon," said my mother, her voice as flat as a wind-swept prairie. My sister had recently had surgery to mend a badly broken leg, and I knew any surgery ran the risk of seeding a blood clot, especially in the leg. A blood clot could block the lungs, cause a stroke, or lodge in a major blood vessel. "They took her to the hospital, and she died."

The words rolled through my brain and took all semblance of order with them. I groped for words, asked for details, and struggled to comprehend the enormity of losing the woman who was my closest biological and emotional link in the world.

I cancelled dinner plans and spent the evening crying and trying to choke down some room-service food. My sister was dead. My sister. Dead. The words kept rolling around in my mind, threatening to batter and destroy all of my carefully collected ideas about death and dying. I had counseled others about the power of death and the permanence of the soul. Death was the other side of life that created a sacred whole. "At least I have some spiritual understanding of death," I consoled myself, "which I'm sure will make the grieving process easier for me than the rest of my family."

That arrogant assumption haunted me over the coming years. As the numbness passed, anger replaced it. Why my sister? And where the hell was she? I expected to sense her in my daily life, converse with her in dreams, and generally continue to interact with her on "other levels." True to form, though, my sister exited quickly and cleanly. She was never one to linger or tarry. No doubt her Aryan energy had catapulted her onward . . . to what?

Even my assumptions about past and future lives evaporated in the volcanic eruption of her sudden death.

I was no longer certain what happened when someone died. Many times I thought of Ron Evans, a Chippewa-Cree teacher who shared a story about a native woman, raised in boarding school by Catholic nuns, who returned to Ron's reservation to discover her roots. She visited one of the elders, hoping to glean answers to spiritual questions from her own tradition that were as definitive as the catechism of her youth.

After a barrage of questions, she delivered her most urgent query last: "What happens when we die?"

The elder looked taken aback. "How would I know?" he asked. "I haven't died yet!"

I haven't died either, and up to that moment I had never looked death so directly in the face. What surprised me most was that death was expressionless. No joy. No tears. No judgement or celebration. Death was not masked, but rather faceless, smooth and unblemished.

Almost five years have passed since my sister Ruth's death. I have felt her presence only once, in a dream about Christmas Eve at the church we attended in our youth. Slowly I have come to new understandings of our voyage through and out of this life. I no longer believe that we have "life contracts" with specific entry and exit dates. I believe we have several points in our lives when we have the opportunity to leave, stay, and/or transform. I see now that my sister, with few worldly encumbrances, was ripe for a quick and easy exit. I am reluctant to wrap explanations or conjecture around the experience of death. I want to leave space for the Mystery to inform me, in its ruthlessly magnificent way, about the mechanics of death.

Nothing Changes When We Die

– AN INTERVIEW WITH –

Thomas Berry

What happens when we die? It must be a pretty intimate question for you as an elder.

Berry: In a certain sense. For me it gets less and less a part of my thinking. It's a case that nothing changes, in a sense, when we die. We enter a new place of our existence that is beyond description. It's a deeper mode of participation in what you call the great celebration of existence. But its greatness is in its specifics. We have a feeling, in a sense, of how to approach it, how to deal with it. But how to describe it – it doesn't easily permit itself to be described in a technical way, it's a mythic likeness that we understand.

Do you think individuality still exists after death?

Berry: Yes. Christianity has a clearer perception of that, I think, than other traditions. The idea of the uniqueness of individuals comes from our efforts to understand the person in Christ. There's a saying in the earlier tradition that the individual is beyond, is inevitable. The individual is beyond analysis because he belongs to that unique something which isolates a person into being an individual, of having a unique identity. The individual is unique, irreplaceable, it cannot be replaced, it cannot be confused with anything else. It doesn't go into anything else. Because there is a certain negative aspect of individual, something like genetic coding. The genetic coding is what cuts off the species from other species. And that's why the species is fertile among their components, but does not reproduce with any other species. The individual person has unique values. That is, in some ways, the great contribution of Christianity. That's why the basic belief in Christianity is not in Jesus exactly. We were not baptized in the name of Jesus. We were baptized in the name of the Trinity. So the Trinity is the basic Christian doctrine and Christ becomes the human manifestation of the second person which is identified as the Word of the Intelligent Being of the Divine. So the idea of a transcendent personal deity created the universe distinct from, not separate from, but distinct from itself is the basic context in which Christianity comes and why there is a certain balance of earth-oriented religions. But that's what gets us into trouble because we begin to fail to appreciate that the universe is not an extrinsic creation. It's a manifestation of the Divine, but the Divine is not distinct from but intimately present in creation.

So when we die, if we're talking about a persona of death, our persona remains?

Berry: That is the basic Christian belief. A very distinct, powerful Christian belief, that the individual survives as an individual. Because we are unique beings, we need the resurrection of the body so that in Christian belief, the resurrection of the body is demanded by the belief in the integrity of the individual person. I think St. Thomas says we are not a complete person until the resurrection of the body. We have a great demand for body. What a resurrected body would be, is anyone's guess.

In terms of our present view of the universe being twelve-billion light years across, where would this body be?

Berry: If the material of one body is transformed into the material of another body where would that body be – Reincarnation. My guess is you will find the answer to this question a challenge.

There Is No Death, Just a Change of Worlds

- AN INTERVIEW WITH -
Brooke Medicine Eagle

What is your notion of death? What is your feeling about what death is going to be like for you?

Medicine Eagle: As our wise ones remind us, there is no death, there is only a change of worlds. If, in fact, we understand that we are eternal, then we know that the energetic presence of ourselves never dies. Yet sometimes we need to let go of this body/personality complex for our own good. One of the Dawn Star's teachings is, "You need sometimes to die in order to trade in your old beliefs and limitations. There isn't any other requirement that you die." We get so caught and patterned, so tied into a certain rooted way of being that it serves us to release the old form completely. A useful function of "death" is to release that old self.

I believe that birth is probably one of the more challenging things humans experience. Coming from that Great Wisdom, the unlimited heart of all things, into a restrictive body – birthing into a challenging world with who-knows-what parents is probably the most formidable transformation we face. "Death" is the most glorious and wonderful possibility. In that process we have the opportunity to open ourselves and release all limitation – to be welcomed into the arms of Love and a radiant experience.

That experience is one of moving up to a broader perspective and receiving guidance that asks, "How did you do with this one? Before you incarnated, we, together, set up some lessons and possibilities; we chose for you magnificent gifts. How did you do with what you were given?" Thus we have an opportunity to consciously look back, to do a life review. One of the more challenging things about death for most of us is that we would look back and go "Oh, golly, I didn't do so well; I didn't use what I had. I was fearful. I didn't trust life. I held back. I didn't give my loving heart or my best energy. I didn't fully express my gifts. I didn't use myself up. I only used 20 percent of myself or 40 percent. What a waste." I think that would be a hard thing to look back at, although I'm sure we have a pretty good sense of humor about it all at that time.

It must be a radiant, almost unbelievable kind of joy, to move out into a more open, unrestricted, welcoming, joyful experience – to be totally bathed in Love.

Will we still be individuals after death, have our own personas?

Medicine Eagle: I have a sense that we can retain a connection with the past life personality, that mind-set, especially as we focus back. However I think we very quickly open out to our eternal soul which is much larger than that limited sense of our self. Perhaps we'll be able to recall every lifetime we've had throughout the eternity we've experienced, giving us a broader sense of ourselves than we had. Much of this is paradoxical and impossible for the logical mind to understand.

I believe, because of the bond of love, that we keep forever the connections with those we have loved, those who remain on earth and other realms. In that way, it seems, we must retain an awareness of individual consciousness. The soul, having experienced all of our lifetimes, evidently still maintains that awareness. I have learned that we maintain connections of Love throughout time. What we carry into the future is what we create through love and only that. It is very interesting to me to think that we might, lifetime after lifetime, come back with what some people call a "soul group." Some of the teachings I have received lately make me think that's possible because Love does connect us together, and if we love each other we could come back in many roles in these Earth plays/lives to help each other learn our lessons. We could be someone's enemy, friend, mother, father, child, cousin, workmate – who knows? It seems very possible that we would enjoy coming back with those we have bonded with through our hearts.

One of the challenges we have, though, as we "die," is the actual transition. One of spiritual practices among many religions is that, for the first forty days of that transition, our prayers should be with them. We should be sending love and support and energy to them in a very focused way. Because the challenge is that the transitioning person may continue to carry old beliefs and energy until they awaken out of them, it is very helpful to be sending them lovek assurance, support, and positive energy. From Eastern religion comes a very powerful chant. It is said at least eighteen times as the person transitions and is repeated throughout the forty days:

"Never the spirit was born.
The spirit shall cease to be never.
Never was time; it was not.
End and beginning are dreams.
Birthless and deathless and changeless remains the spirit
forever."

What a wonderful reminder!

To explain further, let's say that I think that I am going to hell; this is the kind of fear that is very rampant in our society. Although that is in no way required, that's how I will feel and be for a while as I transition out of my body. The great light and Love that shines through will eventually awaken me, yet I may spend some certain amount of time hanging out with the old limiting and fearful beliefs because what I believe will be instantly true when I step into the other realm. It would be very easy to be caught for a while in that wounded belief; it may take a little while for the universe and love to shake me out of that, to get the larger picture. Ultimately all of us will have that radiant experience of unlimited love and being.

It sounds like you have some belief in reincarnation?

Medicine Eagle: Yes, I very much do. If one accepts the fact that we have eternal life, then after a life of sixty, seventy, eighty years, am I just going to sit in contemplation of God? I sense that what we really want to do for eternity is much more creative than that. I believe that we have many, many, many experiences and that they are in many realms in the universe. Certainly, in order to learn some of the really profound lessons we're willing to learn, I do believe we come again, again, and again to Earth. I think that Earth is one place in the universe right now where there is a lot of excitement, a lot of intensity, a lot of possibility for learning the lesson of love and the magic that the heart presents. One of my teachings is that we can incarnate into the future, the present or the past. Many of us right now came in from the future, a future that is a golden incredible time in which we have transformed our world into a more loving and peaceful and whole world. We are coming back, bringing that remembrance to help set that dream in the ground of this present day – to help us move forward in a good way.

Is there a point at which reincarnation will cease?

Medicine Eagle: I have a sense that it will not cease like, "Okay, you can't do that anymore," as a rule. It may be, however, that we have accomplished all that one can accomplish on this sweet Earth and may have other very interesting and exciting things to do and places to go. Shamanic teachers that I have had say that Earth is the sweetest place. If we want a little taste of sweetness and the challenge that brings, then perhaps we come in again and again in a random fashion. I have no idea, but I certainly love the Earth. I love her sweet greenness and the rain on this wonderful morning. At this point I would like to come in occasionally and participate in the beauty of this wonderful planet, especially as she ascends into a golden time of peace and radiance.

What Happens to the Spirit When the Flesh Lies Cold?

– AN INTERVIEW WITH –

John Fowler

What word do you use beside death?

What happens to the spirit when the flesh lies cold? Of course, a biologist or mortician could detail the decay of tissue and the cessation of bodily functions. However this is not the spiritual question. What happens to our spiritual and mental capacities when our physical form ceases to function? I have always avoided the term *death*, not from intimidation, but rather because my experience does not know finality in any form. Experience has taught me that change is a constant. Even at the time of *death* our consciousness is changing and shifting the focus of its attention. No longer concerned with the day-to-day comings and goings, a new horizon appears and upon it a new light from a new east. As we go forth to meet it we are fascinated by our new feelings. This is much like our physical universe where, when change takes place, structures do not simply disappear out of existence – they give birth to other forms. The sun will, after another five or so billion years, have given itself up in a gigantic ten-billion-year-long conversion of helium into solar energy – four million tons a minute of transition whereby a gas is converted to heat energy. One of its side effects is the emergence of life on Earth, my life on this Earth, a life improbable because of my uniqueness, and a life irreplaceable simply because of its unique position in space/time. Here, in this continuum of energy and transformation, we find an exemplar of change, a movement from energy to a matter uniquely conscious, from greater to lesser light, from a mighty, self-sacrificing yet diminishing luminescence, to the growing light of our awareness. In this way, life recognized, organized, revealed and illumined its own consciousness, gave it a place to be, to grow and nurture an unlimited sense of gratitude.

So again, and finally, what of death? Death, as the terminal event of consciousness, is the belief that we are either separate from God or, more strongly, that there is no God and that, accordingly, we can *die* but God cannot. As our cosmologies move towards the recognition that our universe is omni-creative and omni-intelligent they move closer and closer to mapping the stages of my own awareness of the Divine. As is true of my meditative experience and waking revelation of Divine Union, these new universe stories tell me that I can no more be truly separate from God than I can be separate from the universe that sees through me, that speaks through me, that lives through me. Indeed, it seems increasingly clear that whatever union I experience with God must be magnified beyond number by that union which Divinity experiences with our universe.

There Is Choice in Our Beliefs

– AN INTERVIEW WITH –

Virginia Froehle

What about after we die?

Froehle: It is easy for me to understand agnosticism and why people don't believe in God or life after death. No one can prove or disprove either belief. We choose to believe or not to believe. I choose to believe in a Divine Mystery, in a loving, mysterious presence that we usually call God. I also choose to believe that we go on after this life, though I don't know how that will be. I know that who I am is more than just the cells in my body and I believe that "moreness" will continue in some way.

What do you hope?

Froehle: What would I hope for in an afterlife? My imagination is limited. I would hope to experience what people have told us after having near-death experiences – to be encompassed in Light and Love. I would like to continue to be an individual in the afterlife, but if death means melding into the goodness of the Divine, that would be OK. I choose to trust that, whatever the will of the Loving Mystery, it will be for good.

We Reenter the Web

– AN INTERVIEW WITH –

Joanna Macy

What are your images of death and what happens after death?

Macy: We reenter the web. The life that is in us started far before our physical birth in this lifetime. You don't need rebirth doctrines of reincarnation to believe this. It's just a fact of evolution. Every atom in every molecule and every cell of our body goes back to the primal Flaring Forth. Just as in our mother's womb we relive all those many earlier chapters of our life, we have gone through many forms, many birthings and dyings. This is just one more dying, not to be feared.

In the Gaia meditations that John Seed and I put together from our correspondence in *Thinking Like a Mountain*, we talk quite explicitly about this. We acknowledge that all of us have been in human form only recently. In our long evolutionary journey of life, we have taken more ancient forms than this. Countless times we died to old forms, let go of old ways, allowing new ones to emerge. In each time, each worn-out cell was recycled. I was just looking up a great quote, "Think to your next death. Will your flesh and bones go back into the cycle? Surrender. Wonder your weary being through the fountain of life." Even before it comes, death can function as a liberator. It can free our courage and firm up our will and fire up our insight because it helps us let go of clinging to outgrown ways of seeing, and thinking and acting. Death work is included in my longer deep ecology workshops.

So when you die, will you still exist as a person, as Joanna Macy?

Macy: No, except for a while in the memories of people who knew me and, I suppose, through what might remain of my writings. I am not really Joanna Macy either. From the Buddhist perspective that name is only a convenient convention to refer to this ephemeral phenomenon – the Buddhist image of self is as fire – or a flowing stream always changing. In my understanding, strengthened by spiritual practice, I see myself dying into each moment anyway. Nothing stays the same. We practice dying into life to live more fully at any point. I don't believe a particular soul that's in me now is going to continue when my body goes back to Earth and air, fire, and water.

My thoughts are also shaped to some extent by the poet Rilke, who sees our death as a fulfillment and fruit of our life. Do it well, do it fearlessly with loving awareness. Death is totally non-separate from life. I may be scared and want to hang on, but I would hope I step across that threshold with gratitude for the enormous gift of life.

CHAPTER SIX

Where Are We Going:
A Universal Perspective

Keeping Pace With the Creative Spirit

– BY –

Diarmuid O'Murchu

In evolutionary terms the answer is obvious: *We are going forward, lured by the new future that the Creative Spirit always opens up for us!* Patriarchal culture tends to be preoccupied with the past, emphasizing the need to honour and preserve tradition. Preserving a tradition is the surest way to destroy it because the whole of creation is imbued with the power of Spirit and we cannot calcify or limit that proactive, creative power. Moreover, the Spirit blows where she wills, and that usually means a few light-years ahead of the human mind at any particular stage in its evolutionary unfolding.

How do we keep pace with the creative Spirit? By honoring the great story to which we belong in its cosmic, planetary and human trajectories. We know how God works in creation, and God's fidelity to that process over billions of years is itself our greatest guarantee for the future.

Of course, it depends on our ability to see: to see the large landscape and the deep meaning, to see with wholeness and in an enlightened way, to see with the contemplative gaze that honors the complexity and greatness of the divine, and not succumb to the reductionism and minimalism of patriarchal institutions. Evolution thrives on the paradox of creation and destruction. In the evolving pattern there are dips and hollows, great extinctions, which sometimes last for millions of years. Paradoxically, they seem to be part of the divinely ordered pattern, baffling and confusing though they are to our rational, logical minds.

Yet, creation always wins through, and I suspect always will. Fortunately it is not dependent on us humans, although I believe we have a unique contribution to make, especially at this time, in co-creating the new wave of consciousness emerging in our world.

And where will it all end? I suggest we have more than enough to engage the heart and imagination without worrying about endings. Endings are a type of human preoccupation; I suspect the divine life-force is not that worried about endings. In the realm of the living, strictly speaking, there are no endings. Subatomic particles are not destroyed, they are transformed; every feeling, thought and sentiment is absorbed into the collective unconscious and will be reprocessed to build the envelope of global awareness; nature seems to have an endless capacity for renewal and recycling. We ourselves, in the process of our dying become pan-cosmic rather than a-cosmic.

In the basic language of thermodynamics, energy is never lost; it is held and used in another form – sounds very similar to the statement of St. Paul: God never withdraws the gifts that have been given (Romans 11:15).

In a world engrossed in pessimism and often verging on despair, we need to be advocates of enduring hope. This is not the same as the utopia promised by modern consumerism on the one hand, and evangelical religion on the other. It is the hope born out of struggle and engagement, sustained by evolutionary imagination, and nurtured by communities of resistance and prophetic vision. It is a dream based on gratitude for all we have received from our creative God, coupled with an acute and proactive awareness that making the world a better place is the co-creative task to which our God calls us all – now and for the future we create together.[1]

---

[1] More on this topic in my book, *Evolutionary Faith* (Maryknoll, N.Y.: Orbis, 2002) pp. 94–108

(Three Questions)

– AN INTERVIEW WITH –

Brian Swimme

How did life as we know it come to be?

Swimme: There would be a variety of interpretations possible here; I'll give you one explanation. When the earliest life-forms first came about, they generated their own food. The sun would activate chemical interactions in the oceans, which created a number of molecules, and these molecules consumed by the life-forms, but after a while, there was not enough food for all the life-forms. The life-forms would have died off if not for a mutation event that enabled life-forms to actually capture sunlight. This is way back 3.5 billion years ago, and it is really a feat.

Light's moving at 186,000 miles a second and a life form has to capture a piece of it. But the even trickier part is that light comes in chunks called photons, and when you touch a photon to capture it, it disappears. Amazingly, life-forms fashioned a molecular net that, when it captures the light, actually transforms its shape and holds it until it needs energy, at which point it goes back to its original form.

Are you talking about photosynthesis?

Swimme: Precisely. This is an amazing moment in the development of life on the planet. And what's even more amazing is that great moments like this are remembered genetically-they become part of the DNA which is passed down. So right now we have lots of creatures that can draw in sunlight. Look at the way in which the human eye captures light; it uses the same type of molecule that was invented 3.5 billion years ago; it's exactly the same process.

I use this as a way of seeing how the universe remembers what is valuable, what is important. What is retained is the beauty of a particular life. In death we don't leave the universe. We become part of it again – this is the traditional doctrine of the communion of saints. We become part of a huge community.

Where does this leave the doctrine of the resurrection of the body?

Swimme: I think the resurrected body is coextensive with the cosmos; it isn't a loss of identity, it's actually like a new hue or a new tone.

Similarly, the presence of the resurrected Jesus in a certain sense is everywhere. It's still a focused identity; yet it's coextensive with the entire cosmos.

Excertped from the *Loretto Earth Network News,* Summer 1997, pp. 8–9.

The Cycle Continues

– BY –

Debby Brown

We know what happens to the physical body after death; it is broken down, transformed into food and byproducts that nourish other forms of life, and so the cycle continues.

We also know that at death, electrical impulses, which existed in life are no longer there – no brain waves, no electro-cardio impulses. And we know that energy can neither be created nor destroyed, only transformed. Now, what if what is called God – or mystery, or spirit, or whatever – is a field of pure energy? In our present bodies, we are plugged into that energy, much as a lightbulb is tapped into an electrical current. When we die, we become unplugged, but the energy field still exists. All life is plugged into this field at different points or wavelengths. In that way we are all part of the whole. Time becomes relative, depending upon the location of the contact point. As the molecules, or atoms, or other particles of our bodies are broken down after death, they are recycled into another life form, so the contact with the energy field continues, but changes frequency.

This energy field is on a linear path, transmitting in a constantly lengthening field. Therefore, it is possible to tap into what we call the past, but not the future, because the field has not stretched that far yet.

A Continuous Flowing
Energetic Process

– AN INTERVIEW WITH –
Edgar Mitchell

What happens after death?

Mitchell: A process recently discovered, which we're still investigating, is called a quantum hologram. At the bottom of all matter there is simply emission and a reabsorption of energy, quanta of energy. The quantum model of matter isn't little Ping-Pong balls connected by Tinkertoy sticks, such as the drug companies use to sell their new chemical models. At bottom, there are no little Ping-Pong balls that represent matter or atoms. Matter is fluctuating, flowing, emitting and reabsorbing energy. It's a continuously flowing energetic process. And mind you, no one really knows what energy is, we are only able to give it a name and mathematically get some of its properties. We don't really know what energy is except that it makes things happen.

Recently discovered is the fact that these emissions from all matter, what are considered as group emissions, carry historical information about the object. That is now a validated reality. It's been demonstrated with functional magnetic resonance imaging (FMRI), and it has to deal with the non-locality and the quantum correlations of the spin of atomic matter. We don't know a whole lot about that yet, but in quantum physics it's called *non-locality*. It's called *quantum entanglement*. It has this distributed property of coherence, like laser-light coherence, and it seems to be carrying the history of all physical matter. I have written a paper on it called "Quantum Hologram: Nature's Mind." (If you want to take a look at that paper you can get it off my website.) This model seems to support that the experience of a living body, or any bio-matter, is carried in this quantum hologram and is perpetuated nonlocally throughout the universe. In other words, it's a field effect. You can use that to explain virtually all psychic experience. You can use it to explain reincarnation if you like. I say in my lectures quite often, that using this model makes it impossible, in principle, to tell the difference between an old soul and a new soul with a long memory. It's just information. You can resonate and pick up information of a prior life which seems to be your personal information, which is fine, that's what past-life regression is all about. As a therapy, it doesn't really matter whether it's information that helps you with your current life or whether it is indeed your actual prior life. That's a moot point. But, this model (and I don't claim this model is the end-all and be-all of models; I merely claim it's a model that fits the data), this model would say that the experience of a lifetime survives the lifetime, and is available in nature to subsequent conscious beings that can resonate with that information.

Will there be a persona?

Mitchell: Well, let me ask you this: What is a human be-ing, besides the physical body other than the compila-tion or historical record of everything that has happened to it?

So, what you're saying, in essence, is that it could be that there is a certain persona.

Mitchell: My study of thirty years does not support that view. People thirty years ago asked about life after death or consciousness after death. I said, "Don't ask me that question." Until I understand what consciousness is, I can't possibly know whether consciousness survives death or not. You're asking the wrong question. We have looked and looked and looked for the so-called homun-culus or the little man in the brain that drives the sys-tem and we can't find it. So the best answer is that con-sciousness is a process, not a thing. The ancient traditions said the soul is a thing, some*thing*. No, it seems to be a process, and a part of that process is this perpetuation of information in nature. Now, does that support con-sciousness as we experience it now? No, because it seems that the process requires a living organism and this non-local process involves information, feedback and a quan-tum hologram. That is where the research is at this point. All the answers aren't in yet.

And they may never be?

Mitchell: They may never be. But we seem to be getting a much better and closer picture from our new understanding of quantum processes as we apply them to bio-matter and living stuff in consciousness. Now let me tell you why that is true. All of the work within the last twenty to thirty years has shown that consciousness process has properties of non-locality, which means ubiquity throughout the universe. It doesn't propagate $1/r2$ like electromagnetic radiation. It is not screenable with a third Faraday cage as electromagnetic radiation is. That's when we arrived at the conclusion that the only theory that has such properties is quantum theory. So, you are led to believe that something is going on in the brain body even though classical science says that the brain is too hot to support quantum processes. Much of the research over the last decade says that classical scientific view is just not so. That's what we are dealing with. Roger Penrose at Oxford, Stuart Hameroff at the University of Arizona and a whole host of other researchers are saying quantum consciousness is involved with quantum processes in the brain. And that is what my research has shown.

Images of Death

– BY –
Judy Piazza

Maybe it is no accident that I waited until after September 11, 2001, better known as 9/11, to write about images of death. Maybe it is no accident that I write just at dusk, when the veils between the physical and spiritual realms are thinnest. And it seems perfect that I write in anticipation of tonight's full moon after praying a drum prayer that the lunar grandmother would change the tides of ecological devastation, human despair, and atrocity just as surely as she changes the tides of the sea – rhythms of the natural world that are as constant as the cycle of life and death.

Tonight, as the trees begin to turn colors and the crickets are singing their last hurrahs, I have something to write on death. While we mourn the lives of thousands and the loss felt by their families, while we become more aware of the feeling of terror and fear that has plagued other countries relentlessly, while I cringe at the waning light on both sides of the day, while we prepare flowerbeds and gardens for their sleep time, I can write about images of death, and life.

From this vantage point, I see death as a garment for the Spirit, which resides in (but is not contained by) the body. Death is an aspect of the physical body as well as a process that affects the Spirit as well as the body. We dress ourselves in garments of death, just as a newborn is dressed in the colors and clothes of new life. Sometimes we are thrown into the garments of death unexpectedly, even violently. Both life and death are states of being that interact with our spiritual Self, which pervades the body in either state. Our spiritual Self does not require either garment or even the body itself, and is not contained by either, yet it willingly resides in and associates itself with both Life and Death of the body. In this view there is no dilemma in either state of being, in either garment, one being no better or worse than the other. There is only the Spirit that is tempered by both, and given opportunities and choices to further evolve.

The process of death is as important as the process of birth. In fact, the physical dying of the body can actively prepare the Spirit to birth into another realm of existence, free of any physical containers or limitations, in the same way we think of birth labor preparing to bring a new Spirit being into the physical world. The labor of death can be prepared for psychically, spiritually, physically, and emotionally, similar to the labor of birth. Both are valid and valuable "labors," opening doorways into a new form of existence. The process of death and the process of life both require personal preparation (implying that each person's process is unique and non-conforming to patterns of time, place, or behavior). These processes are also both social events that bring people together to question, grieve, celebrate, and reflect on their own place in the wheel of life. And it is this same wheel that governs all species in our expanding universe, clearly demonstrating our connectedness in the ecological web of life and death, and beautifully playing out the natural rhythms and cycles of life, death, and rebirth.

The Cycle of Life and Death

– BY –

Rosemary Radford Ruether

Fear in the face of the fact of mortality and the quest to escape mortality are deep impulses in human beings. Most of the religions of the world have been organized in one way or another around the need to come to terms with death. For many Christians the promise of a blessed immortality is understood as the essential meaning of the "good news." Through the death and resurrection of Christ, we have been saved from death and assured that our "souls," as disembodied individual conscious selves, will live forever with God in "heaven.".…

In order to create a new system of production of food and artifacts to sustain the human community, no longer based on turning wastes into poisons, and poisoning discarded people, we will not only need new cyclical technology, but a new spirituality. Only with a new spirituality that integrates the consciousness of human beings into the whole process of the life cycle of growth and decay, will there be the self-understanding of the interdependency of all things that can inspire the new technology. We need to learn to "think like a mountain" or, perhaps even better, "like a forest." We need to understand the human processes of life, bodily growth, farming, manufacturing, as integral parts of a process by which everything we take in from nature must be returned in new forms to sustain nature.

In order to create this spirituality of "recycling," in which the human life cycle becomes complementary to the life cycles of the plants and animals, air, water, and soil around us, I believe we have to come to terms with our mortality. We must overcome the false worldview that has rationalized our flight from mortality. We will not overcome our tendencies to turn the waste, death and decay side of our life cycle into poisons until we accept ourselves as mortal and learn to reintegrate ourselves as beings that die and decay into the natural processes of renewal of life.

We need to visualize ourselves as an integral part of a dynamic matrix of matter-energy in a continual process of conversation and transformation. This dynamic conversion of the matter-energy continuum has been in continual creativity since the explosion from the primal nucleus eighteen billion years ago. Out of that continual reshaping of matter-energy, the primal building material of earth was formed and gave birth to the processes by which organic beings of ever-greater complexity and capacity for conscious self-reflection have developed.

Although humans are, in one way, the apex, at least up to now, of this process of increasingly complex and conscious organic beings, we, as much as plants and other animals, are finite centers of life, who exist for a season. We too die; all the cells of our bodies disintegrate back into the matrix of matter-energy, to rise again in new forms, as part of a worm or a bird, a flower or a human child. The material substances of our bodies live on in plants and animals, just as our own living bodies this minute are composed of substances that were once part of rocks, plants, and animals, stretching back through time to prehistoric ferns and reptiles, before that to ancient biota that once floated in the first seas of earth, and before that to the stardust of exploding galaxies.

The spirituality of recycling, by which we become interdependent with the positive life processes of all other beings around us, demands a fundamental conversion of consciousness. We have to take into our consciousness and practice recognition of our mortality and transience, relinquishing the illusion of permanence of immortal selves that can be exempt from this process. While this may be a sad word for those who see the individual self as ultimate, it can become a joyful word once we have learned to see ourselves as an integral part of this great matrix of being which is ever renewing life in new creative forms out of the very processes we call "death." One generation of beings dies and is dispersed back into the matrix, so that another generation of beings can grow from its womb. This is the true and only resurrection of the dead. It is the real process of what has been called "reincarnation." As we surrender our ego-clinging to "personal immortality," we find ourselves upheld in the immortality of the wondrous whole, "in whom we live and move and have our being."

Excertped from "The Cycle of Life and Death in Ecofeminist Spirituality from *Creation Spirituality Magazine*, Summer 1995, pp. 35, 38.

"Interestingly"

– BY –

Wanda Hambrick

Interestingly, I believe that "the force," "the power," "the energy," "the source" are words you should use not at all: THE UNIVERSE ITSELF. Nothing more, nothing less. And that theology needs no God, nor heaven to escape to. THE UNIVERSE embraces death, transforming me back into bacteria, earth and continuation of myself in the hearts and minds of those with whom I have interacted. The transcendent is the evolution process itself. That becomingness is my daily life, my planetary time, and the larger bodies of becomingness from which I evolved: Earth, Tiamat, and the Big Bang. I will become the next supernova and eventually the Big Crunch. Why I should be anything more/less than that, when all of the New Story shows this constant transforming over and over and over for everything in, of and becoming THE UNIVERSE, seems a holdover from the classical explanations and no longer part of 20th century explanations for me. (And utterly egotistical that it must be different for us humans!) And the difference in the understandings from those theologies makes a huge difference in my understanding of purpose, cause of tragic happenings, and the living of my daily life. I am constantly puzzled that the New Story keeps being stuffed into the old wineskins of prior beliefs or into new age metaphysics.

Will There Be Any Toads in Heaven?

– BY –

Keith Helmuth

We have a great fondness for toads on North Hill Farm and they seem to have great fondness for us – or rather for the particular environment we have helped shape. There seems to be a direct, positive correlation between garden development and toad population. Toads, of course, are champion insect eaters and we value them as working members of the farm crew. I suppose they must value us as champion insect growers since gardening brings on great blooms of insects as well as vegetables and flowers.

I am concerned about toad populations. According to a variety of recent studies, toad and frog populations worldwide are crashing. Whole species have disappeared from what were thought to be relatively pristine environments. Their disappearance indicates that yet another level of environmental deconstruction has been reached. Ecological collapse is not a fantasy of doom-minded environmentalists. It is happening! Now! Toads and frogs are among the oldest species in the community of life. Their sensitivity to the generalized toxification of Earth's environment is an omen of biblical proportions.

What is going on here? More and more I have come to
the conclusion that the destruction of Earth's biotic integrity has to do with much more than just the overt
necessities of economic behavior. The struggle to center
our lives in creation – in Earth process as we have come
to understand it – it also about excavating the deep psychic structures of the Judeo-Christian tradition, structures which have created our worldview and have driven
our collective behavior in ways that are often antitheti-
cal and sometimes stunningly inappropriate with regard
to the biotic integrity of Earth.

It has come to me that we need to conduct a kind of
archeological dig into the Christian worldview in order
to redeem it from a variety of ecological errors. In my
effort to do this "spiritual" archeology, I have received
particular assistance from the toads with whom we
share North Hill Farm. Encountering toads always
brightens my mood, and good humor sometimes opens
the door on an innovative thought. One summer day a
few years ago, while weeding in the herb garden and having met a toad in the basil, a question popped into my
mind: "Will there be any toads in heaven"?

Now the juxtaposition of such a down-to-earth creature with such a lofty theological concept may seem
whimsically absurd, and, in fact, it was exactly this dissonance which intrigued me. Why does the thought of
toads in heaven seem so incongruous? The answer is not
hard to find.

Looking back over the centuries we see how theological interests have risen and fallen in popularity. One of
the interests which has enjoyed a consistently high profile until recent times is the nature of heaven. Based on

the references in the Bible, an image of heaven has been built up in the Christian tradition which has had profound social, economic, and ecological consequences. Even though, in modern times, it has become increasingly difficult for Christian thinkers to undertake sustained speculation on the nature of heaven, the old image of this promised land has remained a sub rosa component of the Western worldview. It seems, in fact, that the eclipse of heaven as a topic of theological inquiry and general public interest has not diminished the tenacity of the cultural orientation which arises from its history. If anything, the promised land orientation in our culture has grown stronger even as its theological prominence has faded. It has simply shifted from the eternal to the temporal and re-emerged in economics, technology, and social planning.

The idea of heaven derived from the Bible, and developed over many generations by orthodox theologians and preachers, is based entirely on the image of an urban environment – the heavenly city, the city of God. As far as I am aware, there are no rural or wilderness images of heaven in the Bible. The Isaian image of the peaceable kingdom on Earth has generally been regarded as a temporary arrangement. The ultimate goal, the environment of heaven, has always been portrayed as a great and good city.

What is this heavenly city, this promised land orientation? As a package of cultural values, it has a variety of notable features: Ultimate convenience and total leisure. No work, no struggle required. Total peace, joy, and contentment. No conflict, sadness, or suffering. No decline, decay or death. And all this is framed within an entirely urban environment. The concept of the heavenly city is the exact opposite of a rural or wildland life and economy. Nor does it draw on the social and economic arrangements of small town or village life. The concept of heaven, like the design of our central urban environments, is based on transcending the fundamental meteorological, biophysical, energetic, metabolic, and economic conditions of Earth process.

The hold of this vision on the collective imagination of Christendom as it turned into Western civilization, did not wane. It simply moved from the ethereal to the concrete, from the sky to the earth, from theologians and preachers to the political economists, engineers, and entrepreneurs. The whole modern project of economic development – both capitalist and socialist – has been driven by the utopian image of overcoming, through technology, the basic conditions of Earth process, and the establishment of human habitation in an environment which realizes as fully as possible the values and conditions of the heavenly city.

Is this a noble vision worthy of allegiance? Many intelligent persons over the past few centuries have thought so and worked hard to achieve it. Or is it a recipe for ecological and social disaster? A dissenting minority has been voicing this warning. It seems to me the issue is now clear. The roots of the economic and technological behaviors which are poisoning and disabling the Earth are lodged in an image of deliverance and salvation, lodged in a wish for privilege and exemption which starts in the Bible, which has been carried and nourished in Western culture, and has now, through the agency of the capital-driven market economy, exploded in ecologically and socially damaging consequence over the whole Earth.

An image which started with a theological warrant – the image of the heavenly city – has now been translated into a license for bulldozing the ecosystem, undermining the value and dignity of labor and offering shopping malls and theme parks in their place.

If this seems exaggerated, consider the meaning of the toxic, metallic-tasting haze which now routinely overspreads vast regions of our continent and makes public respiratory warnings almost as common as weather forecasts. We are talking about the breath of life. Cancer rates climb. Forest environments collapse. Lakes go dead. Loons diminish. Toads vanish. However we conceive of it – as an urban rest home in the sky or the promised land of total convenience on Earth – the answer to the question of my title is: "No. There will be no toads in heaven."

Obviously, a great confusion has occurred. The attempt to establish the heavenly city of maximum convenience is wrecking the Earth. Somehow we must pull this image – this "ghost in the machine" – out of the driver's seat and put ecological wisdom in its place. I'm not sure what should be done with the idea of the heavenly city. It is a powerful image. Perhaps theologians could issue a recall and try to make appropriate modifications in its character.

Personally, I would not want to inhabit a heaven without toads and since a heaven of total convenience and ease – wherever it is located – seems to rule them out, I vote for a new image of heaven, an image which includes trees and turtles, birds and insects, labor and rest, and plenty of toads. I want a heaven which jumps around my feet.

In the past, those who understood the ecological dissonance of the biblical tradition mostly just ignored it and worked to create an ecologically accurate worldview in the hope of altering the environmentally destructive behavior of modern culture. This re-education is not working, or at least not working fast enough. It appears to me we should now raise the ecologically dissonant elements of the biblical worldview into full consciousness. Perhaps if we can gain a freeing perspective on these elements of our cultural heritage we will awaken the clarity and courage of the changes we need to undertake – the changes of adaptation to the way our amazing natural home actually works and the changes which enable human communities to lift their social relations into a better harmony.

Excerpted from *EarthLight Magazine*, Summer 1997, pp. 18, 19.

CONCLUSION

After almost four years in the process, it is with a profound sense of gratitude that the creation of this book comes to a conclusion.

I have been awed by this undertaking. I have talked with incredible people about incredible topics. Very few people declined my offer to provide their wisdom and insights for this book. It is apparent to me that many people are grappling with these issues, and have been asking the same questions. The development of a new story is beginning.

This book is not a conclusion; it is a beginning. Our changing cosmology is only several hundred years old, and much of it is under a hundred years old, with new discoveries about the universe and the Earth planet happening every day. Conscious human beings who want to lead meaningful lives have a desire to know the answers to these basic questions, "Where do we come from? Why are we here? Where are we going?" Many people cannot accept a new cosmology until we can find answers to these questions, or at least until a new story is under development.

In a culture of so little depth, steeped in meaningless consumerism and materialism, and resulting in behaviors that are destructive to the Earth and its inhabitants, we are in desperate need of a new story. Without it, it will be difficult for the Earth to sustain our species into the distant future. If this book provides some of the elements of the new story, and initiates and encourages new and additional efforts toward developing that story, it will have achieved its purpose.

I would like to receive other writings on these topics. If you have written something, or know of other writings on these subjects, I would love to hear about them. You can send them to me at jschenk@imagoearth.org or by land mail to 553 Enright Avenue, Cincinnati, Ohio 45205.

CONTRIBUTORS

Thomas Berry, CP, Ph.D. founded the History of Religious Program at Fordham University and the Riverdale Center of religious Research. He has served as president of the American Teilhard de Chardin Association, and won a Lannan Foundation Award for *The Dream of the Earth* and *The Great Work*. Together with the scientist Brian Swimme, he wrote *The Universe Story: A Celebration of the Unfolding of the Cosmos*.

Evonn Berube-Reiersen, is employed by Project U.S.E. as an experiential educator. She brings more than one thousand students throughout the year to experience sustainable living and interconnectedness at Genesis Farm and other natural environments. She coordinates the Children's Summer Camp at Genesis Farm.

Ron Bohannon is a writer, artist, lecturer, healer and group facilitator. He has written articles for the *Cistercian Lay Contemplative* (CLC) quarterly publication, member and participant in Creation Spirituality (CS) of Louisville.

Judith Boice, M.D., is the author of seven books including *But My Doctor Never Told Me That!* She is listed in *Who's Who in America*. A Phi Beta Kappa graduate of Oberlin College, Boice has lived and traveled around the world, fostering an understanding and respect for many cultures and traditions.

Miriam Brown, OP is a Sinsinawa Dominican ministering in adult faith anad spiritual development. Since directing the Churches' Center for Land and People (ecumenical, WI, IA, IL) for fourteen, she is program staff and spiritual director at the Racine Dominican Retreat Program, Racine, Wisconsin.

Debby Brown is a former hospital administrator. She has a B.A. in hospital administration but was encouraged to write by her late husband, Craig Brown, who was a professional writer. She has had several short pieces published and is currently collaborating on a novel. A native of Los Angeles, she now lives in Northern Kentucky.

Catherine Browning is a teacher, writer, and contemplative. She holds degrees in anthropology, spirituality, and nursing. She is the author of *Blazing Radiance.* Contact information: Wondernet@aol.com

William (Bill)Cahalan is a psychologist. He leads retreats to help people begin or deepen a practice of opening to the Spirit in nature. His e-mail address is earthawaken2@yahoo.com

Avery Cleary initiated the Hooked On Nature campaign with the guidance of Brenda Morgan, Spiritual Catalyst to ensure all children have an opportunity to develop a relationship with Earth. See more about the program at www.hookedonnature.org.

Mary Coelho brings to her writing an academic and practical background in both biology (M.A.) and theology (M. Div, Ph.D.). She is author of several articles and the book *Awakening Universe, Emerging Personhood: The Power of Contemplation in an Evolving Universe* (Lima, Ohio: Wyndham Hall Press, 2002).

Jim Conlon, Ph.D., is the director of the Sophia Center at Holy Names College. He holds degrees in chemistry, theology, social science, and culture and spirituality. He is a graduate of programs in urban training and community organization. Among his publications are *The Sacred Impulse, Ponderings from the Precipice, Lyrics for Re-creation, Geo-Justice, At the Edge of Our Longing* and *Earth Story, Sacred Story.*

K. Lauren de Boer is a poet, essayist, and editor with a particular interest in ecology, spirituality, and evolution. He is executive director of Earth Light Journal in Oakland, California.

Paul Davies is an internationally acclaimed physicist, writer, and broadcaster, who holds the position of professor of natural philosophy in the Australian Centre for Astrobiology at Macquarie University, Sydney. He is the author of over twenty books, including *The Mind of God: The Scientific Basis for a Rational World.*

Drew Dellinger is a poet, activist, and teacher. A close friend and student of Thomas Berry, Dellinger has given more than a hundred presentations on Berry's understanding of ourselves as part of the story of the universe. (Contact information: 397 43rd St., Oakland, CA 94609; (510) 653-4573; email: drew@soulforce.com; Web: www. soulforce.com.

Michael Dowd, an itinerant evolutionary evangelist, is an author of the 1991 book *EarthSpirit: A Handbook for Nurturing an Ecological Christianity* and two educational websites: www.thegreatstory.org and www.evolutionarychristianity.org.

Duane Elgin, is an author and speaker. He has been in the forefront of exploring humanity's evolutionary journey, sustainable ways of living, and the convergence of the new science with the world's wisdom traditions. He has authored three major books: *Promise Ahead, Voluntary Simplicity* and *Awakening Earth*.

Richard Elliott Friedman is a professor of Hebrew and Comparative Literature and Katzin Professor of Jewish Civilization: Hebrew Bible; Near Eastern Languages and Literatures. *The Disappearance of God: A Divine Mystery* is one of his many books.

Kym Farmer is an educator and consultant. In addition to holding master's degrees both in education and in creation spirituality, she is a certified Montessori and public school teacher. She has written curriculum for teachers on exploring spiritual ideas with children, and on recognizing our place in the larger cosmos. She can be reached on her farm at 4400 Sycamore Hollow, Celina, TN 38551, 931-243-4346.

Cherri Ann Forrest, activated as an interpretive "artist" at age four (multi-media), creates via Rising Sun Studio Work/Playshop & the GeoCelebrate Collaborative (Declaration of Interdependence...)

John Fowler holds a Ph.D. in integral studies. He has been a Montessori director, administrator, and consultant since 1981. John is the creator of the Time Line of Light Cosmological Curriculum for children and adults.

Matthew Fox, a postmodern theologian, has been an ordained priest since 1967. He holds a doctorate in spirituality, summa cum laude, from the Institut Catholique de Paris. Fox is the author of twenty five books, including *Original Blessing, A Spirituality Named Compassion, Passion for Creation: The Earth-Honoring Spirituality of Meister Eckhart, The Reinvention of Work*, and *Sins of the Spirit.*

Virginia Ann Froehle is a Sister of Mercy (Cincinnati region) whose focus is prayer and spirituality. She is a retreat facilitator, spiritual director, and freelance writer. She is the author of the best-selling *Loving Yourself More: 101 Meditations for Women* and *'Tis a Gift to Be Free: Making Choices on Life's Path* (Ave Maria Press).

Gwen Gordon received her master's degree in philosophy, cosmology, and consciousness from the California

Institute of Integral Studies. She is currently teaching at Holy Name University, Sophia Center and the Institute for Transpersonal Psychology, as well as writing a book on evolutionary play.

Marya Grathwohl, O.S.F., is a poet, storyteller, and educator who integrates new cosmology and twenty years experience with Crow and Northern Cheyenne peoples. Her book *After the First Thunder* will be published by Riverhead Books.

David Haenke organized the first North American Bioregional Congress (May, 1984). Currently he is manager of a ecological forestry project in the Ozarks and directs the Ecology Society Project of the Ozarks Resource Center. Writings include the booklet *Ecological Politics and Bioregionalism* (1984), along with a considerable number of articles in various ecological publications.

Wanda Hambrick, a career consultant for twenty seven years, has a B.A. in biology/psychology of human development. Deathing "postgard":1990s/ cancer, 7 including soul-sister, son, husband; prior 1990s/ drunk drivers, 13.

Meg Hanrahan works as an independent media producer and scriptwriter for diverse regional and national clients. Additionally, she is a mother of two who enjoys gardening, hiking and camping, dancing, journaling, and her women's circle.

T. Jack Heckelman was an environmentalist and social activist for more than forty years. He retired in 1988 from a forty two-year career in telecommunications, engineering and management. In 1995 he cofounded the Alliance for Sustainable Future in Pennsylvania. Since the year 2000 he had worked extensively to promote the Earth Charter. Jack died April 24, 2005.

Rich Heffern, a priest in the Sacred Heart Missionary Order and a social psychologist living in London, has lectured internationally and written extensively on new paradigms from a multi-disciplinary point of view. His books include *Our World in Transition, Religious Life: A Prophetic Vision* and *Reclaiming Spirituality*.

Keith Helmuth, is a writer, market farmer, community development activist, and Quaker. He is the author of *Arrowhead To Hand Axe: In Search of Ecological Guidance*.

Kelly Hicks is a spiritual activist who travels the broad triangle of Florida, Virginia, and New Mexico to present ritual and communication.

Marian Honors, C.S.J., is an internationally known artist and teacher who expresses love and care for Earth through her art, gardening, and involvement in community issues.

Paul F. Knitter, emeritus professor of theology at Xavier University, is author of *No Other Name?* (1985), *One Earth, Many Religions* (1995), *Jesus and the Other Names* (1996), and *Introducing Theologies of Religions* (2002).

Marlene M. Kreinin, a visionary poet and storyteller, derived her gratitude for the Earth from interacting with streams, rocks, and evergreen forests as a native of Northern Michigan. She holds an M.S. degree in family ecology and created and taught a path-breaking university course on family holistic health. A coauthor of a textbook *Family Living*, first published by Prentice-Hall in 1982, she has also authored seminal articles viewing social issues and the family from an ecological perspective.

Peggy Logue was the director of Grailville, an education retreat and conference center in Loveland, Ohio. She developed a four-weekend retreat training program to prepare labyrinth facilitators. She has also served as jail chaplain. Peggy is a member of the Grail, an international movement of women, and the Federation of Christian Ministry. Currently she is writing, doing photography and has a wedding ministry. Her article "Meeting Bear" was published in the *Ecozoic Reader* in 2003.

Rev. John R. Mabry, Ph.D. teaches spiritual direction, world religions, and interfaith theology. He holds a master's degree in creation spirituality and a doctorate in Philosophy and Religion. He has served as editor of *creation spirituality* magazine. He is author of: *Faith Styles: A Spiritual Typology for Spiritual Guidance and Ministry*; *God as Nature Sees God*; *Heretics, Mystics and Misfits*; and *Crisis and Communion: The Re-mythologization of Eucharist*. Find out more at www.apocryphile.org/jrm/.

Miriam Therese MacGillis is a member of the Dominican Sisters of Caldwell, New Jersey. She lives and works at Genesis Farm, which she cofounded in 1980 with the sponsorship of her Dominican congregation. She also coordinates programs exploring the work of Thomas Berry, Brian Swimme, and the New Cosmology. Mac-Gillis lectures extensively and has conducted workshops around the world. Contact: (908) 362-6735.

Joanna Macy, Ph.D., is an ecophilosopher and author who brings Buddhist teachings, systems theory, and deep ecology to her inspirational workshops for social activists.

Gene W. Marshall is an accomplished teacher of religion and ethics and is the co-founder of Realistic Living. He has written numerous books, among them: *Good Christian Religion as a Social Project*, and *Christianity in Change: An Invitation to Deeper Dialogue*.

Terri Maue has published poems, essays, and short stories. Her current project is a book of essays, *Walking the Dog: Living by Curiosity, Instinct and Discipline*.

Sallie McFague, Ph.D. is a member of the faculty at Vanderbilt Divinity School and Vancouver School of Theology, and the author of *Supernatural Christians, Models of God* and *New House Rules: A Christian Theology for Planetary Living*.

Edgar Mitchell, Ph.D., was inspired to found the Institute of Noetic Sciences in part by his experience of viewing the earth from orbit. It is Dr. Mitchell's passion to see the scientific proof of the spiritual. Among his books: *The Way of the Explorer: An Apollo Astronaut's Journey Through the Material* and *Mystical Worlds*.

Diarmuid O'Murchu, M.S.C., a priest and social psychologist, is author of several books, including *Quantum Theology, Reclaiming Spirituality* and, most recently, *Catching Up With Jesus.*

Judy Piazza, multi-instrumentalist, recording artist, music therapist, and educator, performs, facilitates workshops on rhythms, songs, and healing sound, travels and teaches internationally. Find out more at www.resonance-andrhythms.com.

Rosemary Radford Ruether, Ph.D. is a theologian and historian. Her publications include *Gaia and God, Women and Redemption, Sexism and God-Talk,* and *Women Healing Earth.*

Peter Russell is the author of several books, the most recent being *Waking Up in Time,* and *The Global Brain Awakens.* More information on his new book on science, consciousness, and God can be found on his website, www.peterussell.com

Janet Schenk is a teacher, social worker, writer, and editor, having worked with children and seniors. The enclosed piece of poetry expresses her belief in and knowledge of "God" as it has changed through life.

John Seed, an Australian rainforest activist, is also an author, filmmaker, musician, and facilitator of experiential deep ecology and "despair and empowerment" workshops.

Stephan Snider is the founding director of Oakland Box Theater in Oakland, California. He holds a master's degree from the New College of California and a bachelor of arts degree from Presott College.

Brian Swimme, Ph.D., is a cosmologist and the author of *Hidden Heart of the Cosmos, Universe Story (with Thomas Berry), The Universe Is a Green Dragon* and the video series *The Canticle of the Cosmos* and *Earth's Imagination*. He is a professor on the graduate faculty at the California Institute of Integral Studies.

Evelyn Pease Tyner is a person, woman, daughter, mother, grandmother, widow, biochemist, perennial student, survivor, friend, and Earth Elder. She is sometimes teacher, seeker, poet, photographer, wanderer, explorer, scuba diver, observer, and prairie enthusiast.

Gail Worcelo, C.P., M.A., is a Passionist nun originally from St. Gabriel's Monastery in Clarks Summit,. Pennsylvania. She is currently cofounding, along with Bernadette Bostwick, a new monastic community—Sisters of the Earth Community—with the guidance and support of Thomas Berry. The mission of this new community is the health and protection of Earth.

Omar Zinn is a homebuilder in Chapel Hill, North Carolina where he lives with his wife, Paige, daughter, Parker and son, Orlando. He still writes poetry and produces music in his spare time.

PERMISSIONS

The editor is grateful to the following publishers and copyright holders for permissions to use the selections reprinted in this book.

Berube-Reiersen, Evonn. *Creation Sprituality Network Magazine*, November/December, 1993.

Davies, Paul. *The Mind of God: The Scientific Basis for a Rational World* (New York: Simon and Schuster, 1993), pp. 184–185, 231–232.

Elgin, Duane. *Awakening Earth* (New York: William Morrow, 1993), pp. 264 and 296–298.

Friedman, Richard Elliott. *The Disappearance of God: A divine Mystery* (Boston: Little Brown and Company, 1995) pp. 236–237.

Fox, Matthew. *Creation Spirituality Network Magazine*, Spring 1996.

Helmuth, Keith. *Earthlight Magazine*, Summer 1997, pp. 18–19.

Mabry, John. *Creation Spirituality Network Magazine*, Summer 1994, pp. 23–26.

McFague, Sally. *The Body of God: An Ecological Theology* (Minneapolis: Fortress, 1993), pp. 150, 156–157.

Radford Ruether, Rosemary. "The Cycle of Life and Death in Ecofeminist Spirituality," *Creation Spirituality Network Magazine*, Summer 1995, pp. 35, 38.

Russell, Peter. *Earthlight Magazine*, Summer 1995, pp. 35, 38.

Swimme, Brian. *The Hidden Heart of the Cosmos: Humanity and the New Story* (Maryknoll, N.Y.: Orbis, 1996), pp. 91–93, 100–101.

Loretto Earth Network News. Summer 1997, pp. 8–9.

INDEX

green press
INITIATIVE

Jim Schenk is committed to preserving ancient forests and natural resources. We elected to print *What Does God Look Like In An Expanding Universe?* on 100% post consumer recycled paper, processed chlorine free. As a result, for this printing, we have saved:

38 Trees (40' tall and 6-8" diameter)
16,187 Gallons of Waste Water
6,510 Kilowatt Hours of Electricity
1,784 Pounds of Solid Waste
3,505 Pounds of Greenhouse Gases

Jim Schenk made this paper choice because our printer, Thomson-Shore, Inc., is a member of Green Press Initiative, a nonprofit program dedicated to supporting authors, publishers, and suppliers in their efforts to reduce their use of fiber obtained from endangered forests.

For more information, visit www.greenpressinitiative.org

Jim Schenk has a Master's Degree in Theology from the University of Dayton, and a Master's in Social Work from Case Western Reserve University. In 1978 he and his wife Eileen Founded Imago (www.imagoearth.org), an ecological education organization, oriented to discovering how we would live if we held the Earth and Its people as sacred. He and Eileen are part of Enright Ridge Urban Eco-village in Cincinnati, OH, working to create an ecologically friendly urban neighborhood. (www.enrightridgeecovillage.org)